SAMURAI Bride

ELOISE SCOBLE

SAMURAI
Bride

INSPIRED
PUBLISHING

Samurai Bride
First Edition, First Impression 2020
ISBN: 978-0-620-87564-6
Copyright © Eloise Scoble

Published by:
Inspired Publishing
PO Box 82058 | Southdale | 2135
Johannesburg , South Africa
Email: info@inspiredpublishing.co.za
www.inspiredpublishing.co.za

Table of Contents

_____

Dedication

I dedicate this book to my parents, who have given me the tools needed to write it.

To my father, Alexander Scoble, whose love for the Word of God, and revelation in teaching it, has spurred me on to also seek personal revelation, and whose creative spirit has set alight those same things in me; whose encouragement keeps it burning.

As my pastor, I remember these words of yours that has kept me a truth seeker: "Just because I preach it up there from the pulpit, doesn't mean that you should just believe it; you need to examine the Word for yourself and let God reveal truth to you. Don't be lazy. Read.

Test."

To my mother, Blanche Scoble, who has inspired many of the stories in this book; your personal faith has, and continues to astound me and your wisdom has always been a guide for me. You have always directed me to my knees.

You are yourself a story teller, and a witness to anyone who will hear.

You are my greatest cheerleader, prayer partner and friend, who couples your friendship with blunt accountability.

I dedicate this book to my son, Zadoq-Levi, who will never be "a heartbreaker" despite your handsome face and charming disposition.

You are a treasure seeker, and protector of hearts. I dedicate this book to your future, as a prince, forerunner and trailblazer, for a new generation and new breed of men, who heal in their loving, and who take back their role as shield, and pillar and leader.

Furthermore, I dedicate this book to every woman who wishes to regain the pieces of herself that are scattered in what society says she ought to be. I dedicate it to every man, who wishes to understand personal activation of the Favour of God, in who he is called to be.

And to everyone who considers themselves as part of the Bride of Christ.

Acknowledgements

Having an idea, and believing that God gave that idea to you, and then turning it into a book is as hard as it sounds. The experience is both internally challenging and rewarding.

It is for this reason, that my first act of gratitude goes to my personal Lord and Saviour, Jesus Christ. Thank you for speaking to and through me and revealing Yourself to me in ways that made me feel heard and loved and special.

Thank you to You, Holy Spirit, for allowing me to feel your presence, and the sweet aroma of your guidance, as You taught me to wait on you chapter after chapter.

And thank you Father God, for allowing me to eat and be filled on the manifestation of You, as I came to know you as proud Father, and protective Father, and Hero Father.

I will never be the same again as I continue to trust for the desires of my heart.

I want to also thank the individuals that helped make this happen.

To my beautiful son, Zadoq-Levi Alexander Scoble, who inspires me every day to be better and do better, and to leave a legacy for him that he can be proud of.

To my sister circle- Ilana, Althea and Zoe -for cheering me on, and believing that I could do this. For not once doubting the talent that you believe I possess. Without this circle, I would not have stories to tell or colour in my life. Each one of you brings music, laughter and light, but more than that, you have provided the umbrella through the storms, the tissues through the tears, and the chocolate, through the heartache. You are my Holy harem. Each one of you, has taken turns being the Aaron to my Moses, as you continually held up my arms. Together with mommy, you have been my mat carriers.

I wish for every girl, a circle like this.

To the husbands and brothers in love-Shain aka "Boetie", Sheldon aka "Daddy" and "Uncle Chad"- I call you by the names my son has given you because you have become my "council of dads". You have taken collective responsibility of him, and because of you, and "Grandpa", my son will never lack a lion or a king in his life.

I have watched you love my sisters and my nieces unequivocally and sacrificially, and I admire, trust and look up to you.

To our "next-gen".

Abigail- for being obedient to the call and voice of God and being trustworthy with my every prayer request; praying in the mall, in the car, on the phone, whenever and wherever. I am so very proud of the person you are.

Keren-Esther – for your silent strength, and super coolness. To me, you are the epitome of the word 'fortitude'. Our little "Miss Lee", you are a Samurai, a true warrior. Don't ever forget that.

To Mika, Isabella-Grace, Sophia-Rose and McKenzie – thank you for just being born. Your gift to me in this time has been a hug, and a smile, and the excitement of seeing me. Those gifts have lifted the burden and frustration, of what often felt like writers' block.

I especially want to thank my 'parentals'. Thank you mom and dad, for pushing me to be what you have always seen me to be, even when I do not see it, and for dusting me off, and pushing me out there time and time again.

Thank you for loving Jesus. Thank you for serving Him. Thank you for this family that I was born into and for being the kind of parents who gave me Jesus.

Thank you Daddy, for giving our "Manne" a name and a legacy, and always covering the shortfall for us- not only financially, but in terms of a constant spiritual covering as well.

Thank you Mommy, for the stories, the inspiration, and all the" mommy- ing". There is no real word for all the things you do on a daily basis, -and when we're all asleep- that ensures that we can prevail. I'm sure your arms are tired, but without you holding them up, the victories would have been fewer, and the fight prolonged.

Thank you.

I want to thank my eldest cousin, Orlen Joseph, and her husband, Pastor Andre Joseph, who were entrusted with my vision; who prayed me through the storms that surrounded me as I tried to focus on my task at hand. Thank you Orlen, for the messages and voice notes, and for crying with me- and for me- before God. I wish for every single person, a trusted prayer warrior that will go into spiritual battle for you, the way Orlen did for me. You are another reminder of the tree of which I too am a branch.

I want to thank Stacey and the late Gary Lebruh, for always believing that I am "special" and allowing me to believe it too.

To Patricia, Charlene, and all my mothers' sisters, who have in some capacity, been a mother to me, who have prayed for me, and been for me, and stood clapping for me, as I journey at my own pace.

To Sharon, Eugene and the Mace family, who have been a friend to me, and "granny" and "other daddy" to my son. You truly have no idea what being able to come to you means to us. As a single parent, having somewhere to go, where my son is loved and where I am able to rest, sleep, recoup and recover is such a major blessing. I always leave there refreshed and strengthened to once again fulfill all my duties to my son. I truly appreciate you.

Thank you to my special pastor, Joseph Cidraas aka Pastor Jo, and his wife Sophia. You have spoken this book into existence and have reminded me that it was on its way. Thank you so much for your prayers, your support, your love and always being available.

I would like to thank Aunty Cynthia Oliphant, who was my Spiritual Lamaze teacher, and mentor in a time I needed one most. You arrived in a time of transition and escorted me to the other side, arming me with the tools I needed to journey further. I have learnt so much from you and I appreciate and love you.

I want to thank all the people who prayed. Really prayed. For me, for this project, for my son- every single prayer for my son- and for my future. You are invaluable.

I want to thank EVERYONE who ever said anything positive to me or taught me something, or rebuked me, or advised me. I heard it all, and your words meant something.

I want to say a very special thank you, to the dream midwives, Darren and Arlene August, and Inspired Publishing.

I carried this baby for months, and you have helped me bring her into the world. You held my hand, wiped my brow, and helped me push. Then you gave back to me someone I recognized but did not know could be so beautiful. And this beautiful baby I share with everyone.

I want to thank YOU, reading this book.

Thank you for investing in me, and in yourself. Let's walk this journey together and start an uprising on our knees. Let's not wait for stars to align for a great cosmic change, let us be the stars that align for a change in our families, our homes, our churches and our society. It all starts with you.

Introduction

In a world rife with staunch feminism on one end, extreme misogynistic undertones on the other, and the ever prevalent queen bee syndrome, it is difficult to find the balance of who we are supposed to be, and how we are supposed to function within a society that has made everything a gender war.

Samurai Bride seeks to set the record straight and bring honour back to such words as obedience and submission, all the while empowering women to live strongly in their beauty and to add grace to their strength.

It touches on themes of Displacement, Royalty, Responsibility, and Sisterhood by God's design.

This book is not just about feminine wholeness- wholeness within herself and wholeness within her realm of femininity and camaraderie of sisterhood- but also about how we are called to fill the hole, and draw men back to who God has called them to be, by vacating seats that we previously felt compelled to fill.

Although it speaks primarily to the Bride in every woman, this book is also for the man who wishes to understand activating God's favour upon himself, his family unit and his future. There can be no bride without a groom.

The lessons shared are aimed at helping both men and women find their designations and fill them uniquely, highlighting the dire need for seeking and committing to healing.

Foreword

LeAnne Dlamini

"...this wife thing is birthed outside the confines of marriage, but is made to live and thrive inside of it."

As I started reading, this line sprung at me in a revelatory sense. As a woman and as a wife of 14 years, I had believed that the role of the wife was one we assumed just as we embarked on our journey of life with our husbands. Everything about this book describes the woman in waiting as an active role that requires us to be responsible for our growth and reminds us what a precious time it is.

Key insights from The Samurai Bride reveal how becoming a bride, becoming a wife starts before "the one" finds us... Eloise has a knack for poetically and creatively bringing images and familiar scenes that we have all experienced to life through her book. This work is lyrical and the storytellers "voice" is audible, however, and even more significant, it is practical and relatable.

As Christian women, how many times have we not heard the wisdom of the scriptures? We have heard, but perhaps, in some instances, we have not been "taught." Eloise practically teaches and unpacks the phases of healing that we need to undergo to become the whole woman. Her pragmatic approach is every reflection of who she is.

When we first started interacting on social media, her message to me revealed that she was in a dark and heartbreaking space, and yet, here she was reasonably and consciously taking the steps to get the healing and refreshing she needed, despite her hurt. Your work excites me, Eloise, as your writing not only brings revelation from the Throne Room of God to the fore, your writing guides and teaches on what to do in order to actuate the healing we need, so that we actively become the whole women and empowered wives of influence that God intended us to be. Her pragmatism as an author is carried on the wings of her own experiences.

Eloise doesn't hold back. One gets a deep sense of her humility as she candidly teaches from her own experiences. Notably, her writing is from a position of having taken responsibility for her actions and choices and one recognises without question that the level of mindfulness and her journey of mastery of her own life, has created a warrior and a conqueror of circumstance. Her authenticity shines through as she makes no excuses, but selflessly offers wisdom and the kind of Godly advice that can only ever come from having embraced the pain she felt, and from having chosen to grow even stronger from the lessons that it offers.

Eloise demonstrates a well-researched "roles" of us as women and wives. In an era where women are "rising up," but where men are broken, she bravely and confidently reinforces the unwavering power of who women are, but still, acknowledging our role in raising, praying for and honouring the men in our lives. This book brings a wonderful demonstration of women understanding and owning their queen-like worth and designation, without breaking every man who becomes tarnished by the reputations of men who may have hurt them.

She delves into a topic that deeply and unequivocally resonates with me, which is the necessity of finding a sisterhood...a tribe of sisters. I appreciate the wisdom with which she unpacks not only the value but also the consequential role the right sisterhood plays in the lives of all women.

This book will move you to action and it will inspire you to "level up." It will open your eyes to revelation and wisdom and usher in compassion and peace that surpasses all understanding that woman, you truly have been designed to live your life from a spiritual position of power. You will be moved to love yourself as the woman you were intended to be; to forgive yourself and be kind to yourself; you will be moved to love and invest in the sisters and midwives in your life and prepare your queen-like heart for the king that God is preparing for you.

LeAnne Dlamini
Singer-songwriter, Entrepreneur and Sisterhood Mama

Review

Ayanda Allie Payne

This is possibly one of the biggest dilemmas of the modern Christian bride: submission versus feminism.

What is submission and what is feminism? Are the two mutually exclusive or can they coexist? Is submission synonymous with oppression or is it one of the utmost expressions of freedom? Is feminism the antithesis of piety or is it akin to self-actualization?

Questions abound, the greatest of which is: "What does the bible say".

In order to fully comprehend submission, one should search the scriptures and ascertain what the Creator envisaged when He called on the wife to submit to her husband.

Returning to the genesis of the matter is pivotal, as we live in degenerate times where the concept of submission has been bastardized and used as a weapon to abuse women, dehumanize them and relegate them to second-class citizens.

This is not what God had in mind.

Submission has been perverted, it has become a dirty word; it has been stripped of its dignity and honour, it has been hung out to dry. In a depraved society we no longer recognize the beauty of a covering and the ensuing reciprocity of submitting one to another. We have long forgotten what God envisioned when He created the union of marriage, husband and wife, a rib from the rib cage, equal in value but different in function.

The Samurai Bride navigates gently but unwaveringly through the controversial terrain of submission and gender parity. Weaving together ancient words, a mother's wisdom, personal experience, godly council and even popular culture, Samurai Bride is a relevant and timely body of work.

Riddled with hard views, that are sometimes difficult to swallow, Samurai Bride will either confirm your beliefs, make you question your stance or cause you to abandon your opinions altogether. Either way, it will give you food for thought, which is necessary for growth.

There is no doubt that even though 'Sisters are Doing it for Themselves' (climbing the corporate ladder, thriving in academia and occupying positions of power) many if not most, have an undeniable desire to love and be loved. One need only scroll through the virtual pages of social media to get a sense of the deep yearning of women waiting to become brides. It is a natural need and should never be frowned upon.

Equally, if we keep on scrolling, we will find far too many women – even Christian women – who are buckling under the enormous weight of heartbreak. The pain of relationships gone awry is almost palpable. Clearly, something is amiss and something's got to give.

Not only do we need to heal as women and society at large, but we also need to recalibrate.

Samurai Bride touches on the importance of healing (what to do while you wait for a husband) and believing God while in marriage (trusting in your maker and not necessarily in your husband).

This is a hearty book that is unashamedly Christian in its outlook and should be approached as such. It will no doubt see many a sister gathered around coffee tables, dissecting its many meaty bits.

And dare I say, the modern Christian man would also benefit from this read, they too were given instructions on how to build a successful marriage. After all, this is the foundation of a healthy family and the very fabric of a prosperous society. When we heal as individuals and our relationships mend, our society will soon follow suit and will have no choice but to be made whole.

So here's to happy, healthy and godly marriages.

Ayanda Allie Payne
Communicator, Community Development Practitioner and Host of Zuri (ZuriTV & Trinity Broadcasting Network Africa)

Review

Darren & Arlene August

Anyone who has experienced our coaching services would have heard me say "A great book doesn't just happen; it is engineered". When I make this statement, most times I am referring to the author putting in all the work to craft a great story, including great elements that will resonate with the reader, and then finding ways to make the book appeal to the ideal reader. While Samurai Bride ticks all these boxes, I remain completely in awe at how this book was simply "Engineered" by The Author of Eloise's life. Her journey, with all of the hills and valleys has produced lessons we believe will empower generations to come.

Throughout the process of working on this book with Eloise, we couldn't help but think of people who would benefit so greatly from the message she shares. The raw vulnerability with which she shares and the timeless wisdom she imparts can only but push anyone who reads this book to pursue better and be more. Real, authentic, insightful, deep and profound are all the words that spring to mind when trying to describe this beautifully crafted message which not only challenges the status quo, but also offers many opportunities to reflect, introspect and guide one to make better decisions – Godly decisions.

As we all strive to be that spotless Bride of Christ, we are excited at this tool which will aid so many in becoming the women and warriors God has destined them to be – even in the face of abuse, rejection and shame.

Congratulations to Eloise for being brave enough to step up and take up the sword to lead the battle of becoming the better bride.

Darren & Arlene August
Founders of Inspired Publishing

Chapter 1
PROMISE

When I was about 15 years old, I sat in the window nook of our rented holiday apartment in Plettenburg Bay, feeling very sorry for myself. It was our annual December family beach holiday, and it was raining outside. My elder sister's boyfriend (now husband) had come along, meaning I was minus a friend, minus a holiday buddy...

When I was 12 years old, after enduring an unnecessary 7-year traumatic event, I had vowed to myself that I would never get married, a vow I had made because of my disdain for the male species. The only 'good man' I knew was my father, and I sincerely doubted a repeat performance in any other male.

Now, only three years later I sat in a window, depressed, and counting the drops of rain as they slid down the windowpane. I had my pen in my hand, along with my journal, and, as I always did, was writing my thoughts, when God spoke to me. His voice was as audible as a human to human conversation, like two people sitting across from each other. I cannot tell you how God started and how or why I so naturally responded, but what I do remember, are the words He told me to write down:

"Your husband will be the crown of men because of you. Your children will be ministers in My house and your marriage and your family will be a ministry." That's what I wrote, and I believed it immediately with no second thought, and no effort of any kind to make it happen.

The years passed by, life happened, and even though I seemed to be no closer to the fulfilment of the words I heard God speak that day, I still held onto them. I knew I would be a wife and mother. I knew it was all I wanted to be. I believed with all my heart that this thing God had promised me was to bless me, and to bless others around me. If God was going to speak this personally to me, the same way He spoke to Moses, then I knew that it could only be good. The only problem was that I didn't feel 'good'. I didn't feel like a blessing. Marriage consists of two people, and one of those would be me.

Despite my sense of unworthiness, I didn't have any other vocation in mind. I knew that every worthy career had its years of tutelage to wade through so, to me, this chosen 'career' was no different. I knew that it would require study and effort and intention. I knew that it would require sacrifice and certain disciplines. But unlike in the days of old, there are no immediate finishing schools to teach ladies how to be a wife, or to teach young mothers the fundamentals of parenting. For some reason, in this modern society that requires qualifications, certificates, and degrees for everything, we think that we can leave marriage and parenting to chance; we think that we can entrust it to some inward manual that will instinctively appear as a guide in our subconscious when the time comes. I don't believe this. I have never believed this. I guess I just didn't trust that, as tainted as I felt, I would find the tools hidden in this broken vessel to love a man without prejudice from a past that wasn't his, or to raise a child to be whole and healthy.

So began my journey of preparation.

Although my journal entry about that promise had never said anything of what I needed to do or be for these things to take place, I felt that because it was spoken to me, the instruction was implied. And since God was the instructor, I went to the Word.

There is a natural, Godly order to everything because, as you've heard it said a million times before, God is a God of order. The intended order for this family thing goes like this: wife and then mother. Many of us, including myself, have reversed that order. Many of us are moms already, but thanks to the grace of God, receiving that kind of marriage that is heaven on earth, has not been ruled out for us. We just need to activate the wife within.

Proverbs 18:22

Whoso findeth a wife, findeth a good thing and obtaineth favour of the Lord. (KJV)

He who finds a wife, finds what is good and receives favour from the Lord. (NIV)

Find a good spouse, you find a good life – and even more, the favour of God. (MSG)

He who finds a [true and faithful] wife, finds a good thing and obtains favour and approval from the Lord. (AMP)

Four versions of the same scripture.

As I read these over and over again three things jumped out at me from each version.

1. Wife / Thing
2. Find
3. Obtains Favour

Without considerably weighing what this scripture was telling me, I immediately began feeling that getting married didn't seem up to me at all. I seemed to have no control over it, no matter how much I willed it so. It was up to chance and whether a man found me 'worthy' of being picked. After all I wasn't lost, so finding me wasn't the issue; picking me, choosing me – that was the issue. As I pondered more on finding ways to get around that, short of proposing myself, those words wife / thing kept staring me in the face as though I was lacking understanding of the most obvious truth.

And just like that, GOD spoke as clearly as He did the day I sat in the window in Plettenberg Bay. "He who finds a WIFE, finds a good thing; not he who finds a girl looking for a ring."

That was the key. *Being* a wife was the key to unlocking this scripture, and more than that, a wife was a THING, not a person. It dawned on me that a woman doesn't magically transform into a wife the moment she says "I do" or as soon as that ring is slipped onto her finger. Not even that enchanting kiss that seals the union, as the minister says "You may kiss the bride" turns the girl into a wife, like it did the frog into the prince. So why, through all these years and all these generations, did we assume that this is how a woman became a wife in the biblical sense of things?

Chapter 2
WIFE

We know that marriage is a union of two people – one husband and one wife. The wife being the female counterpart to the husband. There is no marriage without a husband, and there is no marriage without a wife. Both are needed. The two people in this union are given new names. They go from woman to wife and from man to husband.

"Do you take this woman to be your wife?"

"Do you take this man to be your husband?"

From that moment on, heaven sees that couple as one entity. These two beings become one living, breathing, functioning organism, living in this incarnate state called marriage.

But what is a wife?

If a man obtains favour by finding a wife, it would seem that the writer of this psalm was referring to a designation, a vocation, and not a person per se. What does that mean? Well that means that just because a woman can be a lawyer, and a lawyer can be a woman, it doesn't mean that all women are lawyers. In other words; becoming a wife is much like becoming a lawyer. It's something you study and it's something you practice, and it's something you develop into, not something you instantly turn into.

More to the point, just because I am a woman, doesn't make me a wife. Just because someone is willing to marry me doesn't make me a wife. In fact, this scripture doesn't merely imply that one has to be already standing in that vocation, it blatantly states it. It doesn't say that he who finds a pretty girl, courts her, falls in love with her, and proposes to her, and makes a wife out of her by virtue of a ceremony, finds a good thing. It says he who finds a WIFE. Not to be confused with 'he who finds another man's wife'. This blows out of the water every theory that says a woman only becomes a wife when a man marries her. It would seem that one can actually walk in this realm, for a period, without that coveted ring. It's like doing your articles.

Now don't get me wrong, I am not advocating shacking up, or pre-marital sex, nor am I implying giving wifely benefits to a man you're dating or – more fitting to today's day and age – a man you're 'seeing' in the hope that he will marry you. No, not at all. The way I envision it, is that this wife-thing is birthed outside of the confines of marriage, but is made to live and thrive inside it. It's like a cell that is born a dot, but evolves into semen, and is incorporated into an egg, and together they make a different living organism that grows into a wholly other organism altogether: something much bigger than the sum of its equal parts.

Yes, there is a way to be a wife, and stand in, and practice in that vocation, so that when you are 'found', the one who finds you is finding a WIFE.

Marriage is meant to be a blessing – the entire thing from beginning till 'death do us part'. But the older I got, the more I saw that too many people were either living in amicable co-habitation, or getting divorced. The cohabiters were separating because the cohabitation had stopped being 'fun' or as 'wonderful' as they had imagined it would be; and the divorcers were getting divorced because the marriage didn't resemble those first few years of in-love euphoria that prompted the proposal in the first place.

I must admit that I have judged many divorcees for getting divorced, simply because they 'weren't happy anymore'. We keep hearing things in defence of that statement like 'marriage is hard', and we are constantly told to walk away from those things that 'no longer serve our happiness'. And that's what people are doing. They are walking away from marriages because they are no longer happy, and because those relationships no longer 'serve them' in the ways that make them feel the way they did in the beginning.

Now, I absolutely agree that relationships evolve and that people do change, but do you not think that an all-knowing God would make provision for these things? And since this same all-knowing God is perfection in Himself, would He not then be a God of prevention rather than cure? Of preparation rather than rescue and resuscitation? The problem, I think, is that we treat the sacred as ordinary and we treat the ordinary as sacred. And marriage is sacred.

I was once a divorcee. I am by nature a diehard when it comes to relationships. I fought for my marriage tooth and nail and yet I still ended up initiating divorce proceedings. I am not making

27

excuses for myself while judging other divorcees; please understand me – I comb myself with that same brush, but there is a huge difference between no longer being happy, and being unsafe in marriage..

No doubt there are many reasons behind peoples' choices to get divorced, but there is nothing God cannot fix if we come to Him wholeheartedly. However, it is also necessary to point out that if your life and that of your offspring are in danger, remember that God is pro-life, so you may need to do what it takes to keep yourself and your children safe.

Aside from the fact of these high statistics on domestic violence, and the all too prevalent GBV (gender-based violence), too many people are opting out of this holy union, or not even daring enter it at all, because of the high rate of divorce, both inside the church and out. This raises the question: if marriage was made by God, shouldn't those belonging to Him have a higher chance at success in this institution?

Hosea 4:6 says *My people are destroyed for lack of knowledge...*

My people, that is, God's people, are being destroyed, demolished, devastated, ruined, damaged, shattered. Why? Because of a lack of knowledge. What does this mean? It means that they are ignorant, they lack wisdom, they refuse to obey, and my favourite translation of this verse says "*...because they don't know Me.*" (NLT) This tells us that there is attainable knowledge and wisdom that one can get to circumvent getting or being destroyed. Here, God is not speaking to or about those outside the folds of His family. He is talking about and to those professing to be His children, the ones who are filling the pews on a Sunday morning, who are raising holy hands in worship but who are just as broken in their marriages as the rest of the world who refuse to acknowledge

Him. We are the ones who ought to know better and be better equipped because we have the Word of God. We have everything we need for right living, and for success in every arena.

This book of the law shall not depart out of your mouth but you shall meditate on it day and night, so that you may be careful to do all that is written in it. For then you will make your way prosperous and then you will have good success. (Joshua 1:8) Our responsibility is to study the word if we are to have success. Whether that be success in our businesses or, more importantly, our relationships. WE determine our success. This scripture clearly says *you will make your way prosperous* and *you will have good success.* Not success of this world, but the kind God deems as good.

The world has the excuse that they do not know God, and that they are ignorant of Him and His ways, but, we, in the house, have no excuse.

*The God Who produced and formed the world and all things in it, being Lord of heaven and earth, does not dwell in handmade shrines. Neither is He served by human hands, as though He lacked anything, for it is He Himself Who gives life and breath and all things to all [people]. And He made from one [common origin, one source, one blood] all nations of men to settle on the face of the earth, having definitely determined [their] allotted periods of time and the fixed boundaries of their habitation (their settlements, lands, and abodes), **So that they should seek God, in the hope that they might feel after Him and find Him, although He is not far from each one of us.** (Acts 17:24-32 AMPC)*

In this passage it is made clear that God is Lord. He made everything. He has already determined everything: when you were born, where you are to be born, the countries and lands you will inhabit, and the day and the place you will die – and everything in

29

between. That includes your marital status, partner, and children. God has not set us up for failure. He has required of us to seek Him in every regard, especially marriage – which is the second most important decision of our entire existence. We cannot blame Him when things fail if we don't consult Him when things start. This scripture goes on to say that, in the past, God overlooked our ignorance. Hosea, in the verse quoted, is speaking in the context of idol worship, but the same principle is true for other arenas. We can no longer cite ignorance when we have the tools to make certain that we do not end up a statistic.

Wouldn't you like to enter your marriage fully equipped, and not wade through these un-chartered waters with only a fifty percent chance of survival? Wouldn't it be freeing to know that no matter what lies ahead, you have the tools and weapons in your arsenal not only to ward off any outward attack, but the inward ones too? That is not to imply that the work is a fifty-fifty split, as if you do fifty percent and he does fifty percent and when you finally meet, it makes up the perfect one hundred percent. No, it's a hundred percent effort from you to be found as a wife. And a hundred percent effort for him to be a husband, so that marriage is what God intended it to be. But it all starts with you. You need to found as a WIFE.

Now, this position does go contrary to the contemporary teachings and practices of feminism, and woman's liberation, but TD Jakes once said, that "woman are doing it for themselves and therefore, by themselves."

I have been in a number of long term relationships and I never felt any closer to being a wife, no matter what efforts I made to be the perfect girlfriend. I was even married at some point and glowed with pride at being called "my wife". I did everything I could to be a dutiful wife – all the cooking, cleaning, baking, homemaking – but I still wasn't living as the wife of promise. Despite all my external efforts, my marriage still failed, and so did a subsequent long-term relationship until eventually I was just a single, independent woman, raising my son as best I could. I realized that there had to be more to this promise than everything I was doing in my own strength. I became tired of doing it by myself so I had to go back to God because what I was being taught wasn't working for me. In matters of the heart – and being a wife is a matter of the heart – I felt it best to go to the Manufacturer, back to origins, back to the law of first mention, and see if my warranty still applied.

Chapter 3
IN THE BEGINNING

In the story of creation, as it is told in the book of Genesis, the book of beginnings, it is said that as God went about creating the world on His six day span, He would stop at the end of each day and say that it was good. God continued this day after day. On the sixth day however, He said two things. The first was that it was VERY good, and the second was that it was NOT good.

God's creation of man – the forming him out of dust and breathing life into him – was very good. The making of man in His likeness and image was very good. It had to be. Man was the closest thing creation had to God himself.

Man wandered the garden and fulfilled his first tasks – working the garden and taking care of it. It was here that God assigned him a task greater than tending to the foliage and greenery of the bush: God set him among the living beasts and let his creativity flow as he named all the animals, but even among these, who had a heartbeat as he did, and who had blood coursing through their veins as he did, he was still alone. It was here that God pronounced that it was not good. It was not good for man to be alone. It was here, amidst all the beauty and power and majesty of all He had created that God decided it was time for Eve. She was what this world had been missing. God knew that nothing He had already made – no matter how colourful, or strong or meek, or fierce or tender or brave – would be a suitable helper to man.

So, as the story goes, *God caused man to fall into a deep sleep and while he slept, God took one of his ribs {or} a part of his side and closed up the place with flesh.* (Gen 2:21 AMP)

I often wondered why God didn't just do what He did with Adam. Why did He hide Adam in a veil of slumber? Why did He close Adams eyes from witnessing Eve's emergence into life? I think He did it so that Adam could discover her. I believe that Adam had already been searching for her in the garden as he tended the plants, spoke gently to the sprouts to grow, moved soil around and softly patted the earth, went down on bended knee, and caught every fragrance, texture, and colour of the land that cradled the architectural ornaments of nature for which he was responsible, and with whom he felt a kinship because he recognized his origin in them. I believe Adam searched for his Eve among the living beasts as he went about naming them: seeing her traits in the strength and submission of the lioness, the homeliness of the robin as she made her nest, the disciplined preparation of the squirrel as it gathered nuts for the winter. All the animals were so intriguing and wondrous, but none of them were the one thing he never knew he always wanted. I believe that it was for this reason that God put Adam into a deep sleep, so that when he awoke, that longing and need to search and find would be satisfied, as he discovered Eve.

HE RECOGNIZED HIMSELF IN HER

I believe that as Adam awoke from his 'surgery', he immediately felt the empty sting from what had been removed from inside of him. He didn't know what it was, but he knew that something was missing. He felt different. Incomplete. As he sat up on that operating table, and began opening his groggy eyes from deep sleep, he saw a shadow that resembled his own. As vision returned to his hazy eyes, there stood God and, beside him, a form he had not encountered in all his walks throughout this Eden kingdom.

There is no record of Adam being told where Eve came from. He could have assumed that, just like everything else – the plants, the animals – God must have spoken her into being, or, just like him, she could have come from the ground, from the dust. But from the moment he saw her, he recognized something familiar in her. Adam looked at this being, and saw, that just like him, she was the image of God. She was the image of... himself. She looked like him. She wasn't bowed down like the animals he had named. She didn't grunt or growl. She had purpose in her eyes. I imagine that as he raised his hand to touch her, her skin was soft; as he took her hand, he could entwine his fingers with hers; as he leaned in to pull her close, her body fit into the cove and curves of his own body. I believe he recognized the blueprint as the being same one from which he was designed. He saw that she was different from everything else God had created, and more than that, he saw that she was *like him*. He saw himself in her. In addition to the physical resemblance, and for the purpose of companionship, he saw himself in her.

I believe Eve looked at him as a child looks at his mother from that very first moment of birth. A look that says, "I know you. I have been living inside you, and have heard your heartbeat, as the thunder of purpose and hope. I recognize your voice." She looked at Adam and trusted his voice, because she had heard it in her slumber of creation. She knew his heartbeat because God had laid her there in that inconspicuous place, while his Spirit hovered over the waters. He had always had every intention for her existence. As Adam walked the garden, she had heard his heart throb with each step he took in line with his vocation. As he talked with God she had felt his cadence increase with excitement as he connected with divinity. As he named the animals, she had felt the calm assurance of his confidence to do as he was instructed, without fear. She knew him. She knew him from the inside. So while her emergence was new to him, she had always known him.

I see that recognition in many young girls. It's that thing we do when we practice our signature with the surname of the boy we have taken a liking to. It seems like nothing, and just something kids do, but it's not. It's the pull of Eve in them, already imagining her husband, already getting acquainted with the thing inside her that is for him.

As Adam looked at Eve, I imagine that the vision of her loveliness took his breath away, and as his eyes settled onto her, and into her, the sense that he had woken up with something missing, was replaced with recognition of who she was. He instantly knew that she came from him, because he saw himself in her. It was for this reason that he exclaimed *"This is now bone of my bones and flesh of my flesh…"* He looked at Eve, but more than that, he saw her, and discovered a WOMAN (Genesis 2:23).

If a man doesn't see himself in you, he will never be able to fully love you as he loves himself. And that is the goal, in respect to our given roles: *husbands love your wives; wives submit to your husbands* (Ephesians 5:22, 25). There is a well-known adage among chefs which states, " You eat with your eyes first". It is quite applicable here as well but has little to do with physical appearance. When a man looks at you, when your potential husband looks at you, what does he see? What is he looking at? Can he see the man he is to become with you? I believe that we ought to reflect two things as Christian wives.

First and foremost, we are to reflect Christ, as we are all ambassadors of Christ, and secondly, we are a representation of our husbands. We either reflect who they are, or we refract who they are. (Make a note of the word 'refract', we will unpack it in a while).

Going back to the Garden: while Eve was still in the rib of Adam, it wasn't as though she didn't exist. She was there the whole time. The only way I can describe this (if potentially a bit offensively) – is as a piece of meat. We all know that the best meat at a braai/barbecue is the meat that has spent a significant amount of time marinating and soaking in sauces and spices. This process causes the tissue to breakdown, allowing more moisture to be absorbed, softening the meat, and resulting in meat that is tenderer and even juicier. That's where Eve was. She was marinating in the beating of Adam's heart during the conversations between him and God. She was softening in his obedience as she eavesdropped (Evesdropped!) on these conversations. She was soaking in the presence of both God and Adam as she was hidden in the body of the first Adam. When she was finally unveiled, she exuded an aroma of the 'spice' she had been marinating in. She exuded God, and she exuded Adam. What emanated from her being was every word God had spoken into Adam – words spoken into his bones, and into his heart. When he saw Eve, she was the physical representation and reflection of those words. In her, he saw all that God said he was.

She was the mirror he needed to be able to look at and into, His promises.

Many of us would have watched the late 90's movie, *As Good As It Gets*, starring Jack Nicholson and Helen Hunt. In the movie, Nicholson plays Melvin Udall, an anti-social, condescending, and downright rude author who lives and works in New York City. Helen Hunt plays a kind-hearted, down-to-earth but down-on-her-luck waitress named Carol Connelly, working at Udall's favourite restaurant. The two form an unlikely friendship that grows into something more as the film progresses. At one point, Carol gives Melvin an ultimatum to pay her a compliment. Melvin, being who he is, is struggling with this, when after a long and almost incomprehensible explanation, he suddenly blurts out, "You make me want to be a better man." And at that, every woman's heart melts. It was the thing woman everywhere hope their men would say to them.

This is your mandate: who you are, and how and *whom* you are marinated in, should make him want to be a better man, because he sees that better man in the reflection inside of you.

Chapter 4
THE ESTHER ANOINTING

Many a woman who has read the story of Esther has been inspired by it, not only as a story of courage and faith, but one of great romance and redemption as well. The symbolisms of Esther as the bride of Christ on one end, and as the hero of her own story on the other, form a complete picture of woman as warrior and woman as bride, but what I would like to draw your attention to is Esther 2:12-13 (AMPC):

Now when the turn of each maiden came to go in to King Ahasuerus, after the regulations for the women had been carried out for twelve months – since this was the regular period for their beauty treatments, six months with oil of myrrh and six months with sweet spices and perfumes and the things for the purifying of the women – Then in this way the maiden came to the king: whatever she desired was given her to take with her from the harem into the king's palace.

This passage talks about the preparation the young women underwent in order to be considered for the coveted position of

Queen in place of the disgraced Vashti, and to be part of his harem. It is interesting to note that they had to undergo *six months with oil of myrrh* first, and then *six months with sweet spices and perfumes and the things for the purifying of the women*. Like me, I'm sure many of you were first introduced to myrrh through the Nativity story, where it is told that myrrh was one of the gifts brought to Jesus by the Magi, or wise men.

SIX MONTHS OF MYRRH (1)

One Christmas my dad, one of the greatest teachers of the Word I have had the privilege to learn under, blew my mind as he explained the prophetic reasoning for the gifts Jesus received at His birth. He explained that the reason Jesus was gifted the aromatic resin of myrrh, was as a foretelling of his impending sacrifice on the cross – His death and burial – as myrrh was typically used to embalm the dead. My dad brought scripture totally to life for me when he connected Jesus' birth and death –and the significance of the woman who anointed Him with her alabaster box – in one drop of sacred oil. It's quite a morbid gift to give a new born, but it was all part of Gods plan- the unfolding of prophecy. John 19:38-39 confirms this, where it is told that Jesus' body was anointed with myrrh and aloes in His tomb after He died on the cross.

Myrrh has other uses: Apart from embalming, myrrh has healing properties, and was also used as an anointing oil and an oil to consecrate the sacred. It was a principal ingredient in the holy anointing oil according to Exodus 30:22-25 (AMPC):

Moreover, the Lord said to Moses, "Take the best spices: of liquid myrrh 500 shekels, of sweet-scented cinnamon half as much, 250 shekels, of fragrant calamus 250 shekels, And of cassia 500 shekels, in terms of the sanctuary shekel, and of olive oil a hin. And you shall make of these a holy anointing oil, a perfume compounded after the art of the perfumer; it shall be a sacred anointing oil."

Although it was mixed with a number of other spices, myrrh is the base of the oil, or the foundation of it.

Typically, there are three types of anointing spoken of in the Bible:

Firstly, there is the *consecration*, or setting apart of sacred items or people to God. This type of anointing signified that the anointed one belonged completely, entirely and exclusively to God. For that reason, any person anointed in this way enjoyed Gods favour and abundant blessing.

Secondly it signified a *celebration of unity*, both horizontally with God and vertically with man.

Behold, how good and how pleasant it is for brethren to dwell together in unity! It is like the precious ointment upon the head, that ran down upon the beard, even Aaron's beard: that went down to the skirts of his garments; As the dew of Hermon, and as the dew that descended upon the mountains of Zion: for there the Lord commanded the blessing, even life for evermore. (Psalm 133:1-3)

Just as a point of interest and fun fact: Aaron was the first priest to be anointed with oil and consecrated in this way, which set a precedent for those who followed.

In addition, myrrh was also used as a *cosmetic anointing* in the form of perfume. This kind of anointing is described in Luke 7:38 and 46, when one would anoint the feet or head of a guest. It is again mentioned in Matthew 6:17 by Jesus when He taught that we should never let people know that we are fasting, but rather *"when you fast, anoint your head and wash your face,"* (NKJV). In essence, He was saying, beautify yourself and smell nice. Anyone who has ever fasted for a significant period of time knows that apart from your energy becoming low, you do start to feel a bit drab, and that shows outwardly. Also, there is this little annoying common side-effect of fasting: the dehydration can cause bad breath. Myrrh was therefore used to mask unpleasant odour, including masking the odour of the decaying body of a corpse, during the embalming process.

In each of these scenarios, myrrh was used to turn something bad into something better, something approachable.

Myrrh, in the New Testament, is often associated with suffering, as in the Book of Revelation. The second church of the seven churches of Asia in Revelation 2 and 3 is called the church in Smyrna. (Rev. 2:8). Smyrna is actually the Greek word for myrrh, and the church in Smyrna is the persecuted church, which is suffering for its faith in Christ. Yet in his letter to that church, John tells them that, in spite of the suffering they are enduring, they are spiritually rich (v. 9) and will receive a *crown of life* (v. 10) which will ensure that this church will not be hurt by *the second death* (v. 11). We tend to only remember the negative side of the suffering with Smyrna, but there is a wonderful, positive side in that Smyrna is rich in Christ and will be spared the ultimate suffering of the unrighteous. This reinforces the idea that myrrh also symbolizes the blessing and favour of God, as mentioned earlier with the anointing.

Thus the primary symbolism of myrrh in the Bible is not that of suffering and death, but just the opposite. It is the symbol of blessing and life. That is its use in the Old Testament, both with the holy anointing oil and with its use as a sweet fragrance in the Song of Solomon.

An interesting fact about myrrh is that it was at one time worth more than its weight in gold. When it is burned as incense, it produces a heavy, pungent scent. Also, instead of evaporating or liquefying, myrrh 'blooms' when burnt. Enough about that for now...

Understanding the uses and significance of myrrh, gives us deeper insight and understanding into the symbolism and reason behind using myrrh to "prepare the bride" as in the book of Esther. Before we can even be considered for the role of suitable bride, many of us need to heal from and/or completely die to various things. The book of Esther speaks of this process as lasting six months.

Six months. It was not a quick, do-on-the-fly, multi-task type of thing. This purification ritual required focus and intention, and commitment. The women were quarantined from the outside world. This speaks of intentional separation: cutting oneself off from external influences and concentrating with purpose and intent on the task at hand.

It is worth mentioning to note that, even though they were separated, these women were not isolated. They formed part of a 'harem'. This is described as the female members of the family; a sacred inviolable place; I would dare to call it a sisterhood.

SISTERHOOD

Ladies, join a sisterhood. A 'sacred inviolable' place; a revered and holy place, where violation is not allowed to enter. A place where bonds are unbreakable because of the standard of women who don't gossip about one another, or shame each other because of their struggles, or compete with one another. This is a place where God- minded women can meet to pray together and to encourage one another and to lift one another up, a place where women celebrate – without jealousy or rivalry – when the king calls one into his chamber, where they understand the need for linking arms and raising voices, and adjusting crowns. The harem is not the place where women whine about their men, or badmouth them for their failures, disappointments, and shortcomings.

We often think that our friends and our 'true circle' are the ones we can go to and complain to about our husbands in a safe space. And although that may be true, the flip side is that, in the harem, woman don't join the chorus.

By this I mean, so often we have one of our girlfriends come to us and say, "You know what my husband did?" and then proceed to unpack the atrocity of the day. While this in and of itself is not a bad thing, as we are to bear one another's burdens, what usually ends up happening is a cackling chorus of woman who agree with *how bad you say he is in that moment*. It's like the scene in the movie *Guess Who*, starring Ashton Kutcher and Bernie Mac – who play Percy

Jones and Simon Green Respectively – where the pair have offended their respective partners and by so doing have sent them off to vent their frustration with their sisterhood. Having eventually found the women's location, the two stand outside contemplating whether or not to enter the hallowed space, and it is here that Percy Jones says this: "You don't understand. They done called all their friends and sat up all night ragging on men. They've worked themselves up into a man-hating frenzy."

That's what the harem has become today. We call it a place of "support", but it's not.

My mom had this saying she often used – probably found in the Bible – when she wouldn't agree with our moanings, that she wasn't going to "strengthen us in our anger or wrongdoing." (*Ek gaan jou nie in jou kwaad versterk nie.*) It often grated on us as siblings because you want your mom to agree with you that your husband is being a jerk (for lack of a more colourful phrase). But that is not the purpose of the harem. I would always wonder why my mom never vented with her siblings about my dad's inadequacies or ever mentioned their disagreements, as I had heard others do. All my mom did was praise my dad's achievements and highlight his strengths. While others spoke of their husband's laziness, or their frustration at some or other thing they failed to do, my mom would brag about what he did for her. The good things. Yes, my dad does have shortcomings, and no, my mom wasn't lying; she just chose how she was going to let others see him.

Don't get me wrong, the harem is not the place to hide your hurt and pretend, but it's also not the place to break down the men in our lives. The harem is the sacred space where women come together and unburden with one another and soften one another with sweet spices when we come from the bitterness of an argument or disagreement with our spouse. We encourage, and help strengthen the UNION, rather than adding fuel to the fire of a woman's anger and hurt.

"Let the word of Christ dwell in you richly, teaching and **admonishing** *one another in all wisdom, singing psalms and hymns and spiritual songs, with thankfulness in your hearts to God."* *Colossians 3:16 ESV*

THE SINGING SISTERS

The harem is a place of correction and alignment. It is a place of comfort. It is here where women ought to admonish one another in love and grace and speak to the frailty of our hurt and frustration, with the anaesthetic of worship, before we come under the knife of The Word.

I remember visiting my grandmothers' home as a child, when the entire family would gather. Three generations, and then four, would fill her tiny two-bedroom home.

The men would sit in the lounge and the women would pile onto her bed, and what started as conversation and an unpacking of the dissatisfaction of work, and home and finances, would turn into the choir of angelic voices, as my grandmother would lead them in hymns from the little red book. Her sweet, high pitched voice would carry her kids, and they would sing until tears streamed down her face; until there was such a peace and calm, and reassurance that filled the room. Then she would take her bible and read from it, speak from it.

This became such a habit, that when she fell ill, few knew that she had lost her sight, because still she'd sing until the tears flowed down, and 'read' the Word over her grown kids. The Word was in her. Whether she could see the words on the pages or not, she still gave the Word in answer to every fear, concern and frustration. It was only when my uncle noticed that the Bible was upside down while she 'read' that we realised.

Looking back, those moments were the epitome of correction and comfort in the harem.

My mother and sisters and I often still practice this.

Every so often, we sit on her bed, burdened with worries and cares and hindrances, and just want to unpack and relieve ourselves by 'sharing' (a female word for the opportunity to complain), but my mom would sing. I have sat with her many times, when advice seemed unforthcoming, and words failed, and all we did was sing from that little red book. I would watch her with her head tilted up to the heavens, and her eyes tightly shut and tears washing down her face. This was all that was needed. A washing of the soul, a disinfectant for the heart.

It sounds so old fashioned to do. So Elizabethan, for women to come together and embroider and play the piano and sing. It's laughable, but there's a lot to learn from that, a lot to gain from that.

Have you ever tried it? Have you ever tried coming together with your girls, and just singing, just worshipping, just praising? It sounds odd, but it's no stranger than pouring a glass of wine and putting on some great chill music and singing along until you feel better.

The difference is that in worship we attract the heart of God. In corporate, partnered worship, we change the atmosphere and our hearts are changed. When we get up from that glorious trance, our situation may still be there, but now, so is the wisdom to deal with it. Instead of anxiety about it, you will have peace, and solutions and a grateful heart that God can and will work with and through.

Five minutes of Praise or worship will do for you what four hours of prayer cannot. It will do for you what hours of complaining can never fix. It will refresh you and equip you.

The harem is a place of agreement and activation. It's your "where two or more are gathered…" space (Matthew18:20)

This space and place of women is your pivotal meeting point, the convergence of the conversations between the power of agreement and the agents of heaven who are assigned to release the words into action….

Again I tell you, if two of you on earth agree (harmonise together, make a symphony together) about whatever [anything and everything] they may ask, it will come to pass and be done for them by My Father in heaven. For wherever two or three are gathered (drawn together as my followers) in (into) My Name, there I AM in the midst of them.

Matthew 18:18-19

This scripture is so loaded.

It sets the rules and ramifications of engagement.

Whenever you gather, wherever you gather and for whatever reason you gather, there are a set of spiritual principles that are automatically set into motion.

Women are pack animals, sooner or later they find themselves gathered in some sort of 'these are my girlfriends' situation and the ever popular 'girls' night out', and a million variations of sisterhood. The entire world over, women have banded together in cliques and groups more so than men.

I have always believed that for everything that God has, Satan has an equivalent but opposite, he uses to lead Gods people astray. He could never create, he can only pervert what God has created. I say that, to say this.

Every gathering is a portal into the spiritual realm. I believe the act of coming together garners spiritual attention. The triune God is big on partnership, agreement and the corporate anointing. Strength in numbers and power in unity. Threefold chord....

Firstly, in the spirit realm, *...**wherever** two or three are gathered...* heaven shows up, whether or not heaven has legal right to operate depends on the next line *"...(drawn together as my followers)... in (into) My Name."* In whose name do you gather? There are really only two options. God and not God.

Anything outside of God first and foremost is an abomination to God. I'm not saying that every gathering should be a prayer meeting, but every gathering should bring honour to God.

If the gathering is debaucherous, drunken, and defaming, you activate agents in the spirit realm. If the gathering is negative and full of complaints and insults, you activate agents in the spirit realm.

If the gathering is uplifting and honouring and wholesome, and nurturing and solution seeking, you activate agents in the spirit realm. If the gathering is Godly and Holy, you not only activate agents in the spirit realm...there I AM shows up. The great God, creator of the heavens and the earth, is there.

I AM..........Fill in the blank. Whatever you need, I AM is...and I AM is there, and He comes with answers and provision.

The second principle is this;

Again *I tell you, if two of you on earth **agree** (harmonise together, make a symphony together) about whatever [anything and everything] they may ask, it will come to pass and be done for them by My Father in heaven.*

This word 'agree' here, is the Greek word 'sumphoneo' which means 'sound together'. It means to agree together, or to agree with one in making a bargain, in making an exchange. You are exchanging your agreement for the fulfilment of your request. The sound you make *together* is what God listens to; is what activates the agents of heaven. This together sound is also what activates the agents of Satan to act on your word. The question then is, when the harem meets, what are you agreeing on? What are you releasing into action? What are you and your "sista's" pulling from the realm of the supernatural and giving hands and feet to in the natural?

Look at who is in your harem. .

The harem is not a place for superficial connections and shallow coffee dates to escape the monotony of your routine, or your 'me-time' away from your husband and kids. Your harem must be a place of purpose, meaning, direction, vision and revelation. It must be a place of deliberate covenant relationships.

We all know the story of Shadrach, Meshach and Abednago. But have you seen the parallels to Esther and her Harem girls? In both cases, these young men- and women- were taken from their homes, taken from their places of familiarity, safety and comfort, to be subject under a foreign king, who knew nothing of their God. In both cases, there were covenant relationships.

The three young boys were covenanted together, by the covenant they made to God, to not bow.

It was a covenant that tied them together. They were in this thing, come hell or high water, together.

Esther too, had her covenant girls.

*'Go, gather together all the Jews that are present in Shushan, and fast for me; and neither eat nor drink for three days, night or day. **I also and my maids will fast as you do**...'* Esther 4:16[a] (AMPC)

We know that they were covenanted because fasting is a matter of the heart. It's not something you are coerced into or forced to do. It's a choice that is consciously made, because it's not just an abstinence from food. It would seem in this passage that Esther made the choice for them, but I don't believe that. I believe that Esther could make that blanket statement because she had faith in the already existing covenant, she enjoyed with them. She knew her girls would stand with her because they knew her heart. Because they knew her God.

The third parallel that we can draw is the intensity and conviction of the covenant and death-defying trust in the God of that covenant.

*"Shadrach, Meshach and Abednego replied to him, "King Nebuchadnezzar, we do not need to defend ourselves before you in this matter. If we are thrown into the blazing furnace, the God we serve is able to deliver us from it, and he will deliver us from Your Majesty's hand. **But even if he does not**, we want you to know, Your Majesty, that we will not serve your gods or worship the image of gold you have set up." Daniel 3:16-18 (NIV)*

*"Then I will go to the king, though it is against the law; **and if I perish, I perish**."* Esther 4:16 [b]

The harem is a place of sacrifice and boldness.

Covenant with women who will walk through the fire with you, who will fast and pray with and for you, and keep standing alongside you, as you boldly walk into your greatest challenges with confidence, knowing there's an army, or your 3 maidens, praying you through it. Surround yourself with women who will keep you from bowing down and bowing out of the anointing to which you have been called; women who will push you to pioneer paths that are considered too dangerous, knowing that once you go others will follow...

Covenant with women who have a tried by fire faith, the "even if He doesn't" faith.

If you are single, find yourself a harem while you wait for the call of your king. If you are married, form a harem with women who will hear your heart but ALSO help you lift your husband up to the King of kings.

My mom and grandmother would always say that your friend is not your friend if they cannot pray with and for you.

Covenant with women, who can pray you through, not just pray with you. Women who will take you through when all you can do is nod or agree.

We appreciate those people in our lives who catch the slack, or fill in the gaps for us, when we can't. You know those women?

The ones who will come pick you up for that job interview to make sure that you get there on time, and unflustered; the ones who bring you a change of outfit because you need it.

The ones who will pick up your kids for you and take care of them until you are able to.

The women who will cook a meal for your family because you are sick. These are the women, who are not just invested in you, but also to all that's connected to you.

I met a few of those women when my mom was diagnosed with stage 4B pancreatic and liver cancer. It was such a hard time for our family, and we were struggling and grieving, and barely eating, but God sent us those women.

One such woman, was my dad's sister Noreen. From the moment my mom was diagnosed, and my family went into stages of dealing, from educating ourselves, trying to plan the next steps, to just trying not to drown in the news, Aunty Noreen was there. She took care of the practicalities for our family. Every single day she cooked meals for us. She didn't make little sandwiches or buy take away. No. Every single day, 14 km away, she stood in front of her stove and cooked excellent meals for us. I believe she prayed over the pots as she cooked. I imagine tasting her tears in the meals as she cried and prayed against the death sentence handed to my mother, but in all that she made sure that while we struggled with this, while my mom had to put her duties on hold, that those duties still got done. My sisters and I didn't have the added burden of figuring out who would cook, and what my dad would eat after a long day at work and an emotionally draining time trying to process his wife's health predicament.

My aunt Ruby was another of those women. She came in and spring cleaned our home; she washed curtains and carpets and windows. She could have hired someone to do it, she had the means to, but she did it herself. She made sure our home was clean and homely and comfortable, especially for my mom's recovery.

My mom's sister Carol also went above and beyond. Aunty Care is the kind of woman to not be involved in family politics and gossip and pretty much keeps to herself, her husband and her offspring. So when she arrived at our home with fresh fruits and vegetables and a top of the line juicer to help amend my mom's diet, we knew that this was God sending in the harem.

Providing the juicer wasn't just a kind gesture, it was a statement of faith. It spoke to a future. When we were uncertain of a future that had my mother in it, the juicer, and the constant influx of fresh fruits and vegetables, were a reminder that there would be a tomorrow, a tomorrow in which my mom would need fresh, healthy meal options. Not only that, Aunty Care and Uncle Peter detoured before work every single morning to bring my moms sisters, Patricia, Lorraine, Bernice and Charlene, to our house. It doesn't sound like much, but they left for work at 5:30am on a regular day. Only now they chose to leave at 5am, so that they could take someone to be with my mom.

My mom's sisters came in, in a steady stream, to be with her while we were at school and at work. They left behind their families and their responsibilities to be there. They sat with her, prayed with her, sang with her and gave her hope. And then they slipped out incognito when we arrived so that we could spend time with her.

My youngest sister Zoe was so young at the time and took the diagnosis as a notice of death. She became introverted and angry and anxious. She was a nervous wreck. We tried to keep everything as normal for her as we could, because despite cancer, and our world as we knew it changing, it wasn't over. Cue Stacey.

Stacey, my cousin, would pick Zoe up from school every day and drop her off every day. On days that my mom was particularly under the weather, she diverted the ride home and took Zoe for ice cream to distract her.

Then came the strangers. People like Sharon Cloete, and Rhema South pastor, Pastor Laurel Cassel who drove my mother to chemo and sat with her. Who cleaned her up after bouts of vomiting, and walked this journey with her.

These are Harem women.

There are many women who made those months bearable, whose names I cannot mention for time, but they were the Harem women. What I want to you to note about these women, is not they supported my mother, but that they came in and took the reigns from her, so that all who were dependent on her, were not displaced. The day to day logistics were taken care of, relieving the family to be able to process and deal.

These women's work kept the work going. Not only did they keep the work going, they also provided hope for the future.

In Exodus 17, we see a similar thing happening in the life of Moses, albeit on a far grander scale. The Israelites were encountering their first opposition while wandering in the desert, being attacked by a group of nomadic raiders known as the Amalekites. While Joshua led the troops into battle, Moses, along with Aaron and Hur, watched the battle from a nearby hill. Exodus 17:11 reads, "So it came about when Moses held his hand up, that Israel prevailed, and when he let his hand down, Amalek prevailed." Eventually, Moses became weary, and so Aaron and Hur responded by holding up his arms until the Israelites were able to finally defeat the Amalekites.

The importance of Harem women is not your typical 'support group'.

These women- the aunts and cousins of my extended family- came in, taking turns holding up her arms. The role of mothers in society is one we know we cannot do without. Mom in the home, is the person we pretty much go to for everything. From knowing where your favourite shirt is, to your deepest heartache, and in our home, it was no different. We needed our mom.

We needed her to do those mother things if our home was to continue functioning, but she couldn't at this point. My mom keeping her arms raised over us, ensured that we prevailed, and had all the tools we needed to succeed in our day to day lives. And when the big C struck, we had a bunch of Aarons and Hur's come in to hold her arms up, ensuring that we could still prevail.

They were not only a harem to her, but proved to be generational and inclusive harem, spilling over to my sisters and I, and even to my dad. They filled the gap by being a mother and a wife in the duties we often call menial tasks, but are the things that kept our household running, and more importantly, gave us the grace and strength to fight alongside my mother, so that we, as a family could beat cancer. And beat it, we did!

In your harem, you will find your roles rotating, in that sometimes you will be a Hur or an Aaron, and other times you might find yourself being a Moses. You need to master both roles, being able to raise the arms of another women so that her family, or her business or her tasks prevail, and also, on the flip side, learning to let go and trust; resting your weary arms in the hands of your sisters so that your family, your business, or your tasks prevail.

Covenant does that. Not friendship, but covenant. Mark 2:1-4

And again He entered Capernaum after some days, and it was heard that He was in the house.

Immediately many gathered together, so that there was no longer room to receive them, not even near the door. And He preached the word to them.

Then they came to Him, bringing a paralytic who was carried by four men.

And when they could not come near Him because of the crowd, they uncovered the roof where He was. So when they had broken through, they let down the bed on which the paralytic was lying.

When Jesus saw their faith, He said to the paralytic, "Son, your sins are forgiven you."

Here we see the story of a young man whom Jesus healed. This was not the first time, nor was it the last time that we see Jesus heal someone, but this one stands out to me, because to me, it's a true picture of the necessity of a Godly harem.

So I know, it speaks of men here, and the "harem", in its definition is a haven for women, but I believe the principles of the harem do apply to men as well, in all its benefits of having a Godly circle of correction, motivation and upliftment.

This one is not a parable; this is Jesus actually teaching in Capernaum and an actual paralytic- a person who has some condition that markedly restricts their ability to function physically or mentally or socially.

The scripture doesn't say much about who this person was, or the severity of his paralysis, but we can assume that it was pretty severe, to be tied to a bed and carried about like that.

It also doesn't say much about who "they" were, that brought him there, but it does speak volumes of the relationship that existed between them.

First of all, they came together. They looked at their friend or brother and decided that not only did something need to be done, to help him, to restore him, to lift him up, but they decided wholeheartedly that it could be done - if he was taken to the right person.

The take aways from this are vital to your core group, vital to your inner circle. And we all need an inner circle.

Yes, we need women who will hold our arms up, but we also need women who will carry us, when our feet also fail.

What does this look like?

My youngest sister, as I said earlier, was hardest hit by my mother's diagnosis, and that anxiety, depression, fear and darkness followed her well into her marriage.

It was not something we saw coming. It manifested itself in rage and tantrums and trembling and uncontrollable and unexplainable fear. While this young couple was meant to be living in their honeymoon phase, discovering one another, they were battling a third party in their marriage that they had no weapons or tools or knowledge to fight.

It was only divine orchestration that saw them moving into my apartment with myself and my 1 year old son only one year into their union. We thought we were doing it to help ease the financial frustrations we were both experiencing, but God had other plans.

During this time, I got to see first hand the strain that this anxiety had wreaked on my sister personally, and on her marriage. I saw her husband try to lift her under the weight of it, but being ill-equipped to do so alone. It was their marriage, IS their marriage, and he was determined to help her through it. But from where I stood, all I saw was an exhausted and exasperated young man, and a frail, unsure, insecure bride, who "didn't want to be this way".

My sister doesn't know it, but instead of sending in the pallbearers the devil had waiting on standby, as he tried to convince her to take her own life, God sent in the mat carriers.

Four women who took a corner and carried.

My mom, my two sisters and I, we started a whatsApp group called "Praying for Zoe".

I almost forgot about that time because God so seamlessly carried her through, but there was a time….

It wasn't just a WhatsApp group. It was a covenant to pray, to take turns praying, but more than that, we fasted, and we carried our sister, our baby to the roof.

We lifted her in worship, we sang around her during Friday evening prayer meetings that she didn't even know was about her. We had "worship evenings" where she broke down, and we let her. We had "worship time" while she was oblivious; in times when she was stiffened to the voice of God because the hurt was just too much, and we broke down for her.

We broke down and cried before God, with the same desperation that the four men had, when they broke the tiles of the roof to get into the room where Jesus was.

As we broke down from the top- from my mother, to my eldest sister, to me, and the third born, we were opening up heaven as Jesus waited below to receive her.

We broke down genuinely to get her to Jesus.

Then we lowered her with words of release, and victory and encouragement, and joy that she was not feeling... and when Jesus saw our faith for her, He forgave her, of herself, and healed her.

Today my sister is a healthy, happy, confident wife, and a warrior of a mother. Things she had convinced herself were not for her.

She could not do it for herself, and had lost hope when it became too dark and paralyzing. She couldn't even find the strength to give it to Jesus, and she gave up, but her mat carriers came and each grabbed a corner.

Be an unnamed mat carrier. Have mat carriers.

A mat carrier's faith will get you healed. A mat carriers faith has weight with Christ. A mat carrier will do for you spiritually, what you are too paralyzed in despair, to do for yourself.

Bring your mats into the harem with you, there'll always be someone to carry.

Now back to Esther and seeking singles, it is in this harem that the purification and beautification ritual takes place. As they were submerged, and drowned in this oil of myrrh, their skin was made soft and smooth and cleared of all manner of scurf.

If you are single, find yourself a harem while you wait for the call of your king. If you are married, form a harem with women who will hear your heart but help you lift your husband up to the King of kings;

For Esther and seeking singles, it is in this harem that the purification and beautification ritual takes place. As they were submerged, and drowned in this oil of myrrh, their skin was made soft and smooth and cleared of all manner of scurf.

This world is harsh and hard, and Satan has done all he can to remove the softness of women, making them stiff and rigid and tough, and calling it resilient and strong. There are too many women who are told that they are alone because "men are intimidated by strong women", as if your strength should disqualify you from the desire for a covering. No. Godly men are not intimidated by virtuous strength. But that is not the kind of strength that women are usually displaying. We have confused strength with aggression and hardness of heart. When a woman is rude and unpleasant and dismissive, and bossy, she tends to label that as strength, but it's not. It's the callous that has grown over the places where she has been hurt. Places that once were soft and supple and receiving, are now dry, hard, rough and unwelcoming. There is nothing that time spent in the sacred anointing can't soften and smooth out. Even the wrinkles of waiting, worry, and time are reversed as God gives back the years that the locust has stolen.

One of the reasons that I held onto a relationship that had already become toxic and unhealthy for me, was my fear of starting over. I could not reconcile myself to having to meet someone new, or sharing my stories again, or ever having to 'put myself out there'. It wasn't that I was scared of rejection, it had to do with the time that might be spent on another wrong person. I calculated my years and came to the conclusion that I no longer had any 'recovery time' left. My coining of that phrase simply meant that I didn't have the time to make new mistakes. I didn't have the time I needed to get over or heal from whatever hurt the next wrong decision might lead to. It was already late in the game, already the eleventh hour. By now I needed to have certain things in place. You know them – the checklist of life: have a husband, buy a house, start a family – all those things that meant stability for me. So it just seemed more plausible to remain in my current mistake and make the most of it.

But that's the thing of it. It doesn't matter how late in the game it is, or how old you are or how old you feel, there is nothing that

God cannot restore and return or turn back. Soaking in the anointing gives back the years. It doesn't just add the years, it gives them back. It restores youth, and virility, and even fertility. It adds quality to quantity. So where you were termed an 'old maid' God will make you a virgin bride. Where life and hardship has aged you and worn you out, the anointing will renew and rejuvenate. It's like botox for the soul.

Now, the scurf that is cleared in the myrrh bath, speaks of flakes on the surface of the skin that form as fresh skin develops below. It is essentially a type of dandruff and/or dry skin ailment. I cannot help but describe it as a shedding of the old skin. This is not a once-off baptism, but an everyday dying to self, and shedding of bad habits and undesirable behaviours; it is a daily practice of immersion in the Word of God until it becomes a lifestyle; coming up out of that 'burial' as a sweet smelling savour in the nostrils of our God.

I will accept you [graciously] as a pleasant odour when I lead you out from the peoples and gather you out of the countries in which you have been scattered, and I will manifest My holiness among you in the sight of the nations [who will seek Me because of My power displayed in you]. (Ezekiel 20:41 AMPC)

If, like me, you are still single in what seems to be the latter years of your life, with dwindling hope of ever being betrothed, you may feel like I did: scattered, abandoned, rejected, exiled, and excluded. God knows this feeling. But there is a purpose coming from this pain. *God Himself* wants to lead you out. Think about that. Think about this great and eternal God leading you out, taking you by the hand, and leading you down the aisle as a father who walks his daughter to her groom. He will personally lead you out of the places where you have been disparaged, lonely, abandoned, rejected and exiled. He will lead you out of this terrible place called 'single and alone', and He will *manifest His holiness* [in you] in the sight of those who will seek Him because of His power displayed in you. You will become a beacon of hope, all the while fulfilling the great commission.

It is at this point that we can completely agree with Ani DiFranco, who sang the opening song to *My Best Friend's Wedding* starring our favourite redhead, Julia Roberts.

She sang:

"Wishin', and hopin', and thinkin' and prayin'

Plannin' and dreamin' each night of his charms,

That won't get you into his arms."

All of that certainly will not bring you to wife status, but neither will the rest of her advice, which I do not whole heartedly agree with:

"Show him that you care just for him.

Do the things that he likes to do.

Wear your hair just for him..."

Or my personal favourite lines to this song: "So if you're thinking how great true love is,

All you gotta do is hold him
And kiss him
And squeeze him
And love him
Yeah just do it and after you do,
You will be his."

Sorry to burst your bubble ladies, but if you feel that you have to work on a trade exchange for that coveted ring, you will not be terribly happy with a marriage that comes from that kind of negotiation. Yes, all of that kissing and holding and squeezing is required, but those are the things he can get from anywhere and anyone. What you need to do, and what I encourage you to do, is to follow the process and find your place in the harem.

Going through this process of separation, purification and beautification, is a beautiful and rewarding thing. It's a place where you learn life lessons, and discard learned behaviour. It's a place where you glean – glow, clean, and learn. Singleness can become a threshing floor of preparation, not a punishment in loneliness. Stop spending your moments wishing you were not alone, or wishing you were married, and start gleaning from the women around you – both single and married. Start being an encouragement. Prepare your soul and your heart. Eliminate what is not of God and that which hinders your heart's desires.

2 Corinthians 2:15 (NLT) states that *Our lives are a Christ-like fragrance rising up to God. But this fragrance is perceived differently by those who are being saved and by those who are perishing.* This new fragrance you will start to give off, will rise up to God. Honouring God in your singleness will alert Him to who you are; it will draw His attention to you. Not only that, I believe it will also differentiate for you between the eligible and ineligible. God wants

to eliminate this dating by trial and error, and wants to bring you to your intended. He wants to help you avoid 'recovery time'. God wants to give His best for us, but He also wants us to be the best for whom He is giving us to. I need to be the best version of who God designed me to be, if I expect God to give me His best. If I deserve the best, then so does my husband. As the saying goes "It's not about finding the right person, it's about being the right person."

Wading through these troubled single waters, and meeting more than my fair share of suitors, I realized how imperative it is to meet the requirements of my requirements. In other words, if I require a man who is financially stable, I need to be financially stable, which in turn means I need to look at working through my debt and bad financial decisions. I can't expect him to marry my debt as well. If I require him to be faithful, I need to be faithful also, which means that I need to practice that in all arenas. Remaining faithful to him in the now, means no casual flirting because I am single, or messing around because I am lonely.

Look at your requirements and match those up to who you currently are, and allow God to work through and with you. This way when you make your list, you don't ask amiss.

SIX MONTHS OF MYRRH (2)

The second thing myrrh did to the women of a harem, especially in those hot countries, was to take away all ill-smelling scents. Whether we like to hear it or not, many of us have 'hot tempers', many of us are a 'hot mess'. Many of us are walking around with heated anger issues, and boiling rage from circumstances of our own making, or of things outside of our control. This rage might be romanticized as fiery passion, but after a while, it just causes a stench that most men want to get away from. It becomes a repelling agent that drives away peace, and, only attracts the irritating, disease-bearing 'mosquitoes' that are attracted to heat and stagnant water. Earmark that word 'peace' – this is something vital. We will revisit it a bit later.

Cool down, calm down, and start walking into a room like a breath of fresh air. Start being the cool breeze on a hot summer's day. Practice being the refreshing rain that ushers in springtime. Be the fragrance that lingers in the air and sets the tone of the atmosphere.

It is said that scent is the most powerful memory trigger. Rebecca MaClanahan said it best when she said, "Of the five senses, smell is the one with the best memory." Why is this important or even worth mentioning? Because the fragrance you exude can take him from a moment of weakness and defeat and remind him how to win. It can remind him how to relax when he's stressed. It can remind him of the strength that awaits him at home, or the breast of comfort that he can look forward to coming home to. In the battle, it can transport him away from the smell of fear and loss.

Deaf and blind American author and activist, Hellen Keller said, "Smell is the potent wizard that transports you across thousands of miles and all the years you have lived." This scent is your morning prayers. It lingers on his clothes, and follows him through his day, and when life becomes too much for him to bear, he can be reminded of what he has already conquered, and refreshed with renewed hope to keep going.

SIX MONTHS OF MYRRH (3)

The third thing that myrrh did for the women of this harem, was to enliven and invigorate them. There are few things as exhausting as being a single woman. The only thing that trumps that, I believe, is being a single parent. You are just worn down all the time. Emotionally, you are trying to keep yourself happy and smiling and 'wear a cheerful countenance' just in case you run into Mr. Right. You don't want him to think that you are one of 'those miserable bitter women' so you are trying to hold onto all your feminine wiles, while having to take care of everything yourself: maintaining a home, carrying out household handyman chores, changing car tyres and everything in between. It's exhausting. God knew it would be; that's why He invented partnership. Adam was without the physical manifestation of Eve for a short while until God said it was *not good*, but Eve was never without Adam. She was made as a helper. Not as a 'do-it-yourself-er'.

So how do you keep yourself fresh faced and toned, and pepped and goal oriented, and independent, while still having an air of vulnerability about you? Get into a harem, where you can be refreshed and invigorated and equipped.

Remember the verse we started with in Esther 2?

Now look at verse 13 (AMPC):

Then in this way the maiden came to the king: whatever she desired was given her to take with her from the harem into the king's palace. In this way... After the work done for purification and beautification *the maiden came to/ was presented to the king.*

She was not presented to unworthy suitors. She was not presented to 'nice guys with potential'. She was not presented to the princes, or noble men, or high ranking officials. No. She was presented to her KING. And added to that, before she even entered his presence, before even an initial meeting with him, she is already given *whatever she desires*. I'd like to phrase that as 'she was given the desires of her heart'.

This whole process does sound a lot like Psalm 37:4 – *Delight yourself in the LORD, and He will give you the desires of your heart.* That's because this is exactly what it is.

I am not a Hebrew, Greek or Aramaic scholar, so I cannot dissect this scripture in some awe inspiring way, but I can tell you how God revealed it to me. I was fighting with Him about a boy. A boy that I desperately wanted to have love me, the way I felt I loved him. I half prayed about the relationship, and half tried to manipulate God into giving me what I wanted – what I considered to be my heart's desire. I desperately paced back and forth in my room, having this inward argument with Sovereignty. "Lord, if I give this over to you, if I 'delight myself in You', all You are going to do is change my heart's desire and make me want something I don't want!" I reasoned and I yelled and I cried. I didn't want to want anyone else. I wanted this one, and I wanted God to change his heart to want me too. As I ranted and raved and threw a-three-year-old-size tantrum, it was as if God was just sitting like a loving parent, waiting for me to stop.

When I finally stopped, He said "Yes, I will give you the desires of your heart. But not as you think. I am your Father; I know what I have purposed for you. I know what's best for you. You may fight Me now, but if you let Me, I will cause your heart to desire a thing, and I will give that thing to you. I will place My desire for you in your heart, and when you realize how much it's for you, you will want it too, and I will give it to you."

One would think that such a personal encounter with God would ease my heart, but it didn't. I cried harder and deeper and just mourned this thing that God was 'taking away from me'. I felt betrayed and manipulated. I wanted what I wanted and wounded

God's heart by acting as though He didn't know what was around that bend, as though He didn't love me as much as He says He does.

There is a difference between something that's for YOU and something that's FOR you. God intends both for us. Something that has been designated and set apart for us, and something that has our best hope and interest at heart. That's the something that says "I got you."

When you delight yourself in God, when you see Gods heart for you, when you celebrate your place in the harem, and when you immerse yourself in the oil of anointing, your heart changes. It is filled with new things, with Godly things, and it is from this place that your wants change. You want what He has purposed for you, it becomes what you instinctively desire, and when you ask for that thing, you will receive it, because you have learnt to ask from the abundance of God's heart, and not from deception of your own. (Jeremiah 17:9; Proverbs 16:25). Your self-worth has changed, and therefore, so will that standard of man you desire and attract.

You ask and do not receive, because you ask amiss, that you may spend it on your pleasures. (James 4:3 NKJV) In the Harem, in the anointing, in the dying to self, and in the healing, we learn what we ought to desire.

THE LIST

The story of how my mom and dad met is one my sisters and I have heard countless times. My dad's version of this story, was that he was just an 'extra', a 'tag along' on his friend's date.

My mom's version is one of purpose and intention. Yes, she too was there as the alibi for the female counterpart of this secret rendezvous, but what was thought to be an impromptu 'blind date', was my mom's date with destiny. Months before this evening, my mom, being the special kid she was, had already logged countless hours in prayer with her list.

My mom had an encounter with God at an early age. While the other kids were reaching their social milestones, she was in prayer meetings with her mom, her best friend, and the other older ladies of the community. And when she wasn't there, she was at choir practice. Always at the church. Always in the house of God. It wasn't for any reason other than her naivety and desire for God that this was her life. She always told us that even before she came to know herself, she knew God. She had known no other life than this.

I think she must have been 11 or 12 years old when she penned the list, but it detailed her desire for a husband. Her main requirement on this list was that the first boy to date her would be the man who married her.

So here she was, 13 years old, on a blind date. My dad didn't stand a chance. This boy would be her husband. She had asked God for a specific thing, and she trusted Him. It was that simple. She didn't stop praying and believing. But she also didn't try to will this boy into the man she wanted. She had prayed it through, and now she had to pray through it. She didn't change her list or even tell him about the list. It literally had nothing to do with him and everything to do with her conversations with God. Something magical must have happened that night, because from that evening on, they were 'dating', in the most juvenile sense of the word.

When her mother, my grandmother, found out about him, she encouraged her to pray even more. When others only saw a hippie with long hair and bell bottoms, my grandmother saw a soul, so they prayed together, believing that this was whom God had sent. My mother held onto her list, and never stopped praying it; after all, only time would tell if this boy would be the man on her list.

I cannot tell you exactly what was on that list as I have never been privy to seeing the actual list, but there were 6 things that she always mentioned in the retelling of this story.

1. The first date thing.
2. He had to have clean fingernails.
3. He had to be light in complexion/ fair skinned (being a dark skinned girl, in the apartheid era, this was her desire).
4. He had to have good hair.
5. She didn't ever want to wash overalls on a Sunday night.
6. He had to be a pastor.

I'm sure there were plenty of other things more noteworthy to mention from her list, but these are what she told us. She had made this list from a child's heart that was filled with a Godly desire for a good husband. Because of her time spent in the Word of God, among the women of God, she managed to tap into God's desire for her and was able to ask for it.

A lot happened after that first night, including a nine month break up that saw my mom running away to Durban – the smartest way to keep her meddling hands from trying to fix it herself. At the end of it all, in December of 1977, she and my dad were married. They entered their marriage, pure and sexually undefiled, and late September 1978, they welcomed their first daughter.

Mom never had to endure dirty, greasy fingernails, and she never in all her life had to ever wash an overall on a Sunday night. Added to that, my parents pastored a church together for many years. My dad hounded many souls into the kingdom, and led many to salvation in Christ. His legacy, not just as a man of God and a man of integrity, but also as a soulwinner, is what I admire most about him. I have attended many funeral services, and thanksgiving services where people thanked my dad for introducing them to Christ.

This is the light-skinned, good-haired man my mom had prayed for at just 12 years old. She had found her place in a harem that consisted of her mom, her best friend – who also married a pastor and enjoyed many years of service to Christ in a beautiful marriage – and the elder Christian ladies, the 'church sisters'. She had discovered God's desire for her, by seeking Him, and had asked from the abundance of His heart for her, and God gave her everything she had asked for. She can always be quoted as telling young girls to 'write their list' as she did, and to pray through it, then to pray it through. It won't always look like what you wrote, but if you keep praying and trusting, and remaining faithful, God will bring it to fruition.

I'd just like to add some twitter wisdom right here and say: "Be as detailed with your prayer as you are with a Roccomama order."

SIX MONTHS OF MYRRH (4)

As relaxing as Esther's beautification and purification ritual sounds, remember the line from the Hillsong worship track *New Wine*.

"In the pressing, in the crushing..."

That is how it happens. Grapes have a very short life span, but wine, from those same grapes, not only has longevity, but increases in value, and flavour, with every year that passes.

In a similar way, myrrh, when burnt, blooms.

When Esther was in her crushing, in her burning, she became the Queen that Israel needed. She bloomed. She didn't shy away from fighting a war for her people that could have been fought in battlefields. No, she bloomed as a diplomat, as a level headed negotiator, as a protector, and as a warrior. It was the crushing and the fire, that took Hadassah from beautiful orphan girl to Queen. Before this moment, Hadassah's defining characteristic, and the thing that got her in the door, was her outward beauty. But after this, we can characterise her as a woman of nobility and strength and courage. She came in as a trinket, but proved to be worth more than her weight in gold.

Chapter 5

THE TWO WIVES

A *wife of noble character is her husband's crown, but a* *disgraceful wife is like decay in his bones.* (Proverbs 12:4 NIV)

I had always understood this scripture to mean a wife who was rude and loud and disrespectful, and dishonouring – the kind of unruly woman who screams at her husband and belittles him in public. I imagined her as an aunty wearing her nightgown and slippers, with a cigarette hanging from her lips and her hair in curlers, yelling profanity at her husband, so loud that neighbours are beginning to gather. That is the wife that disgraces her husband. That's who I saw when I read this scripture, so I believed I was never in any danger of being that woman. But when I read this scripture properly, the Holy Spirit immediately nudged me to understand the difference between a disgraceful wife, and a wife that disgraces her husband. Here's what God dropped in my spirit ...*a disgraceful wife is like decay in his bones.*

Firstly, disgraceful is described as being 'shockingly unacceptable'. If you say that something such as behaviour or a situation, (or even a person) is disgraceful, you disapprove of it strongly, and feel that the person or people responsible should be ashamed of it. So, in theory, it's a shockingly unacceptable wife that is like decay in the bones.

Going back to my earlier statement that 'wife' is a designation, let us, for a moment, for the sake of clarity, replace wife with 'law enforcement officer'. There are certain definitions that describe designations and to fall outside of those definitions, we cease to be those things. For example, a policeman's oath demands that those taking it act with integrity and respect for people's diversity and the law. According to the South African Police Service, the oath below is taken by each member of law enforcement when they become policemen and policewomen:

As members of the South African Police Service we will perform our duties according to the following principles:

1. **Integrity**

   - Application: Employees of the SAPS regard the truth as being of the utmost importance.

   - Explanation: We, as the employees of the SAPS, continually strive to uphold the mission, values, ethical principles and ethical standards of the SAPS. We will behave in a manner that is consistent with these values. We will act honestly and responsibly in all situations. We will always tell the truth, perform our duties with noble motives and set an example in the communities we serve.

2. Respect for diversity

- Application: Employees of the SAPS acknowledge the diversity of the people of our country and treat every person with equal respect.

- Explanation: In performing our duties, we will always show respect for cultural and other diversities in the community. We will treat every person with equal respect and honour their rights as inhabitants of South Africa. We will not unlawfully discriminate against any person.

3. Obedience to the law

- Application: Employees of the SAPS respect and uphold the law at all times.

- Explanation: Our duties mainly involve enforcing the law, and in our application of the law we will always stay within the law and Constitution of our country. We will, at all times, avoid any conduct which would make us violators of the law. We will protect the inhabitants of South Africa against unlawful actions.

4. Service excellence

- Application: Employees of the SAPS work towards service excellence.

- Explanation: We will, at all times, perform our duties to the best of our abilities. Our conduct will bear the mark of professionalism. Our conduct and appearance will be proof of our commitment to service excellence.

5. Public approval

- Application: Employees of the SAPS always work with and for the approval of the community.

- Explanation: We will serve the best interest of the community, seeking the approval of the broad community in everything we do.

However, failure to adhere to this oath, and acting in a manner that contradicts this oath, changes the designation of the badge holder, from one of law enforcer to criminal. So let's bring it home. He/ she has now become a disgraceful officer, a 'shockingly unacceptable' policeperson. Unacceptable means that he/she may no longer call himself or herself a 'law enforcer' but will now go by a new name – lawbreaker or criminal. He may still look like a police officer, still wear the uniform and still carry the gun, but he's still just a criminal. The politically correct term we have adopted is 'corrupt cop' or 'crooked cop'. I believe this term is just our grace factor playing out, leaving hope that he can be rehabilitated to just 'cop' – someone who still honours the badge, and adheres to the oath.

A disgraceful wife may be regarded in the same way – someone who still wears the ring but acts in direct opposition, and in violation of her initial oath and mandate. A disgraceful wife is a woman who has brought shame on the designation. She may not swear, or scream, or show any of the obvious outward signs but she is a disgrace to the designation of wife, to the God-given calling and God designed mandate. Eventually, however, the disgraceful wife becomes the wife who disgraces her husband. Now she extends that shame to his designation, and what once was an internal silent destruction becomes an external annihilation, not only of her designation, but of his as well, and ultimately the living organism called the marriage.

...a decay in his bones

Bone decay only happens after death. Every piece of information I have read on this subject has told me that it does not occur in the living, but only in the last stage of decomposition. Let that sink in. Other translations of this scripture use terms such as 'rottenness in the bones' or 'cancer in the bones', but the Aramaic Bible in Plain English states this *...as a boring worm in wood, the woman that does evil things destroys a husband*. A boring worm is commonly found in dead wood. A disgraceful wife is one that destroys 'husband', one who has silently undermined and subjected him, one who has usurped his role and stripped him of his authority.

I mentioned a word earlier that I would like to go back to. The word is 'refract'. This word gave me chills, and blew my mind all at once, as I went into its meaning. It's described as 'to subject' or 'to alter or distort'. Synonyms include words such as bend, divert, detour, deflect, alter, change course. A disgraceful wife is one that has not reflected the light placed in her, the light spoken into Adam, and mirrored in Eve, but has refracted it, diverted it, caused it to change course. Remember that wife is a designation, and naturally then, so is husband. Because husband has been destroyed or distorted, by the callousness of the disgraceful wife, man runs from being husband. What once reflected him now diverts him. We have come to call this 'commitment phobia', and have resigned ourselves to the fact that many men in today's society suffer from it, but I believe it's the diversionary tactic the enemy used, as his first act to separate. The woman is the gateway to man, and that's why the serpent came to Eve. He didn't choose Eve because she was weaker or because she was more gullible, he chose her because he was planning on 'killing two birds with one stone' – the separation of the unit from God, and the separation of the unit within itself.

Restoration typically happens from the bottom up, building happens from the bottom up. So I believe that if we, as woman, take our place in the Word, we will once again awaken the wife within, and reflect what has been placed in us for ourselves and our husbands. Once we are where we need to be and have vacated usurped roles, the kings will return, and the kids will follow order.

I am reminded of the great Disney classic, *The Lion King*. Nala came to find help for the prideland, and she found Simba. How he had seen himself because of the lie, had become so distorted, that he had gone against his own nature and become a non-hunting, non-roaring vegetarian. It was only once Nala reminded Simba that he was the "one true king" that he looked deeper into his reflection and saw his father. It was here that he was able to lift his eyes to the heavens and finally hear the voice of the great king speaking directly to him, and giving him the tools he needed – courage, faith, and wisdom – to go back and reclaim his throne.

We all remember the scene where Mufasa bellows from the clouds "remember who you are", and the triumph as the tempo increases and Simba runs with purpose to take his rightful place.

I want to put this to you. Your job is not to BE king where there is no king. Your job is to SHOW him the reflection, remind him that he is king and point him to his Father, the Great King. Do this, and watch him rise and roar and make haste to fight for his kingdom. Then don't let him fight alone.

Chapter 6
MIRRORING

I always understood mirroring to occur in a subconscious hierarchy, when the lesser would mirror the more dominant. I may have been wrong, but that, for the longest time, was my definition, and perhaps I wasn't too far from the truth as mirroring is described as the behaviour in which one person subconsciously imitates the gesture, speech pattern, or attitude of another. Innately, we tend to mirror those people in our lives that we admire or spend copious amounts of time with, whether at work, or socially. We essentially see this as just picking up habits but it's so much more. In my research on mirroring, I came across, this in the Scienceofpeople.com.

"Kuhn et. al.found that when someone mirrors your behaviour, the areas that activate are the same ones that process rewards and make you feel good. So not only is mirroring hardwired in your brain, but it is also rewarded."

Michael Yarbrough from Mission.org says that "...Mirror neurons give us the ability to understand each other better, show significance of our relationships and share emotions with other people, building a foundation for empathy."

Mirroring is about being in sync, or getting in sync. The Merriem-Webster dictionary defines being 'in sync' as 'a state in which two or more people or things move or happen together at the same time and speed... The film's sound and picture need to be in sync. Often used in conjunction with 'with', such as 'She moved in sync with her partner.'

Significantly for this subject matter, mirroring allows your husband to see himself in you because of your connection to him, and his dream, because of your emotional and spiritual investment in taking his vision and making it your own. It is essentially about giving up the individuated identity for the identity of the whole. It's merging the two to become one, with one heart, one mind, and one goal.

When we say the two shall become one, we tend to treat it as a conjoined twins scenario, where the two individuals are now tied together in a common area but still have their own mind, own heart, and own ideals, but because of the 'deficiency' of the conjoined area, they are 'forced' to move forward together to get things done. That's why the surgery of divorce, to separate the conjoined area, is often an option. Becoming one is more than the alignment of ideas and goals toward a common, mutually beneficial end. Becoming one is dying to self and being reborn into the new role and relationship, forgetting what lies behind and pressing onto what is ahead. It is not the merging of two like-minded people, more the emergence of one unit functioning in a God-given capacity.

The butterfly is never a caterpillar again, but does not regret the transformation process or the fact that it is now a butterfly. If a woman chooses to remain 'Miss Independent', pushing her own agenda, she chooses to remain single. If she chooses feminism over femininity, she is declaring a war of the sexes, and it's not a gender war. A gender war inevitably displaces and/or kills the husband, and it misplaces the wife. When these two factions are twisted, children stray from their roles and are inevitably lost. Staunch feminism therefore, makes man/ husband redundant.

Although mirroring is not the merging of two individuals into one complete person as is the idea of oneness, it does give us an understanding of the concept, short of literally climbing into the body of your husband. Mirroring can teach us valuable lessons for partnership, communication and connection. I think it speaks directly to Paul's words, "Imitate me, just as I also imitate Christ." (1 Corinthians 11:1 NKJV) The chapter goes on further in verse 3: *But I want you to know that the head of every man is Christ, the head of woman is man, and the head of Christ is God...*This, to me, is biblical proof of mirroring in the marital relationship. In instances of preparing for marriage, the one we need to imitate/mirror is Christ. This passage also clearly states the spiritual hierarchy. It is leadership that trickles down and is not negotiable – one that is under submission of the other. This is not mixed martial arts where we fight for pole position and the strongest contender gets to be on top. Know whom you are mirroring. We learn these traits by practice, and in the absence of a godly husband to imitate, we have Jesus.

For a man indeed ought not to cover his head, since he is the image and glory of God; but woman is the glory of man. For man is not from woman, but woman from man. Nor was man created for the woman, but woman for the man. For this reason the woman ought to have a symbol of authority on her head, because of the angels. Nevertheless, neither is man independent of woman, nor woman independent of man, in the Lord. For as woman came from man, even so man also comes through woman; but all things are from God. (1 Corinthians 11:7-12 NKJV)

Woman is the glory of man...

When we look at the above scriptures, we tend to see only the limitations and restrictions imposed on woman, and how they are to be subject to man and every misinterpreted scripture that has led us to believe that God sees woman as less than man. But I want you to know and understand that you are man's glory. Glory is used to describe the manifestation of God's presence. You are the manifestation of God's presence in the life of your husband.

Read that again.

You are the manifestation of God's presence in the life of your husband. Isn't that the finding of a good thing? You are the portal God uses when He wants to show Himself. Manifestation is when something spiritual becomes real, or tangible, or quantifiable. But are you really? Can you really say that you honour this role in such a way? Glory is also praise, honour, or distinction extended by common consent or something that secures praise or renown. Yes, you are indeed a trophy wife. We have frowned upon that phrase because we have diminished the power of our words. We have taken it to mean a compensation for a lack or a loss, but a trophy is a decorative object awarded as a prize for a victory or success. In ancient Greece or Rome the weapons of a defeated army were set up as a memorial of victory, and this was their trophy. Anything serving as a token or evidence of victory or achievement, of valour, skill, or success is not a negative thing. You are a walking talking representation of your husband's victories. You are decorated with bravery and should be flaunted and celebrated. You are the symbol of everything he has conquered because you prayed for him, because you stood in the gap, because you *are* wife.

A trophy is not easily attained, and not everyone in the fight gets one, but God has awarded you, His Princess, to the mightiest man of valour. This is not a strange thing. In 1 Samuel 17:24-25 when David takes food to his brothers who are cowering because of the Philistine Goliath, we are told that the king's reward to anyone who can defeat Goliath, among others, would be the hand of his daughter. It is pertinent to note that *all the men of Israel, when they saw [Goliath], fled from him, terrified.* (v.24) ALL but one. It was to the one man who stood and fought and emerged victorious that the Princess was given. You are that Princess. God, the Great King, is not going to award you to just any person. No, you deserve a proven man. A warrior. A hero. You deserve someone that sees attaining you as a great measure of success, because he knows what he had to go through to get you and therefore knows your value. Yes. You are indeed a trophy wife.

Chapter 7
HELPMEET

For this reason, a man shall leave his father and mother and be united to his wife, and they will become one flesh. The man and his wife were both naked, and they felt no shame. (Genesis 2:24) It is here, in the very next verse, after Adam sees Eve, and calls her WOMAN, having seen his part in her, that Eve went from 'woman' to 'wife'. But what qualified her? It was the very reason for her creation. She was a helpmeet, suitable to Adam. Eve was made *for* Adam. And added to that, the two were one flesh. God elevated Adam above all that He had created, giving him dominion as far as he could imagine, but then broke him down to build Eve up.

Eve's Place

I've heard it said that a woman ought to know her place. And there are so many ways to interpret this, first as sexist, then as domineering, and also as limiting, to mention but a few. But let's for a moment, forget the tone and space in which it is often said, and finally ask, as woman, where is my place? Truly and sincerely.

*** WARNING!!! Non feminist, non-girl-power content ahead.***

Over the last while, I have been noticing an increase in feministic, girls-rule-the-world, I-am-woman-hear-me-roar, content being made available. Whether that be in the form of female empowerment seminars and talks, songs with strong deterministic girlisms and undertones that exclude or displace man, or T-shirts with gender dominating logos and slogans. There are more and more female lead and female-dominated cartoons, such as Nella the princess knight, Elana of Avalor, Sophia the first, Frozen, and Moana etc. Our little girls (and boys) are being flooded with an influx of 'woman-doing-it for- themselves' material. To be fair, it is a stark contrast from what we grew up with: Cinderella, Snow white, Sleeping Beauty, and Rapunzel, all damsels in distress, locked in the darkness of eternal sleep or pseudo death, waiting to be awoken, resurrected, and rescued.

I am not at all saying that these newer animated characters are to be rejected and scoffed at, but it does beg the question, why is there no middle ground? Why are we only either helpless, hapless maidens, forever in distress, in desperate need of a man, or single warriors who fight the wars of men, not needing a man? Is it just me, or are there others like me, who don't really fall into either category? I have heard the beautiful, poetic analogy, as I'm sure you have, that woman, in her creation, was not taken from man's feet, to be beneath him, or from his head to be over him, but from his side to be next to him. And I do believe that, yes, it is that simple. A woman cannot be alongside, in such close proximity to or in partnership with a man with whom she is at war; and she cannot be of service to a man whose sole purpose is to continually awaken, resurrect and rescue her.

Did I just hear a quarry of woman gasp in utter horror and disbelief... "Be of service to a man"??? Yes, be of service... 'a helper suitable to Adam' 'a suitable helpmeet' remember? For some reason we have taken that word 'helper/servant' to be a swear word, as if it's the height of blasphemy. You can call a woman a ton of dirty derogative words and she'll find a way to own them, but call her a servant and a helper and she's ready to shank you. Why is that?

When purpose is not known, abuse becomes inevitable. When purpose of a role is not known, the power and influence that that role yields is subject to abuse. To quote the words of Blogger Theoneste Ted Ngiruwonsanga, "When you do not know the normal use (purpose) of a thing [or role] you will abuse it. Abuse is actually gotten from the words ABnormal USE." Abuse then, is using an item or observing a role for anything other than its intended purpose.

Abuse does not only come from external sources, but can also be projected from within. You abuse yourself, do yourself a disservice when you take on the role of the man, even in menial tasks, in an effort to prove that you are equal to, or that you don't need a man. Replacing the role of man, leaves the role of the wife vacant, and ultimately displaces the children from that union. So in essence, all three roles are left empty and vacant, while we scurry around trying to find our identity.

Just because things are a certain way and have been so for a lengthy period of time, doesn't make it right. We can train our little girls, as we've been trained, that we don't need men. And we can teach our little boys that they are dispensable in this 'the future is female' era, but the universe – and all its God-given workings – will never align to it. It will always be rejected in the spiritual realm, and there will always be a war for re-alignment, an imbalance that needs to be corrected. Please don't misunderstand me. I am not saying that a woman is 'incomplete' without a man, or that her purpose is found solely in him, because both those statements reek with blasphemy.

God made woman complete, lacking nothing, just as He made man, and added to that Ecclesiastes 12:13 states, *All has been heard; the end of the matter is: Fear God [revere and worship Him, knowing that He is] and keep His commandments , for this is the whole of man [the full, original purpose of his creation, the object of Gods providence, the root of character, the foundation of all happiness, the adjustment to all inharmonious circumstances and conditions under the sun] and the whole duty for every man.* So it is clear by this portion of scripture coming from the wisdom of King Solomon himself, referring to all humanity as 'man', that a woman's sole purpose was not to please man, but to fear God and keep his commandments. On the flip side however, Eve's honour to God came in the form of her honouring her role toward Adam.

Now I want to reiterate, that not every woman has to be a wife, but in accordance with Biblical law, it is a prerequisite to things like having sex, or becoming a mother. Unfortunately, we have drifted so far into complacency, and a 'God will understand' stance, that we have sought to unravel the entire structural integrity of the family dynamic to soothe our loneliness.

This book is not for those who choose to remain single and live a life of abstinence; they may choose a path that to them is more worthy, which is also why convents exist. But God only gave us two options: Marry or remain single.

We gave ourselves wiggle room, with fornication, and living together without the nuptial blessing, and even choosing to have children outside of their God-given right for a covering, with sperm donors, and civil unions, calling all of these makeshift collaborations a' family'.

I am not bashing single parents. As I write this, I am a single parent, but I know that had I honoured my first point of purpose, which is to fear God, and seek first HIS kingdom and HIS righteousness, then all those things for which I longed – marriage and children and family and a good life – would have been satisfied by Him because He would have *added all those things unto me.* (Matthew 6:33) Many – not all – but many single parents are single parents for the very same reason: loneliness, which leads to sin.

I am not bashing joined or blended families and step families either. There exists a dire necessity for step moms and step dads, because biological moms and biological dads stepped back, leaving an empty space, and room for those worthy to step up. Even death has left spaces that needed to be filled, so there is really no judgement.

But that is an entirely different conversation...

Again, I will say that this book is for anyone not wishing to remain single – and by single I mean 'unwifed'. If being a wife is something you are interested in and are seeking, read on.

Chapter 8
ELEMENTS OF A WIFE

B reaking down the elements found in a wife led me to where she came from. We already know that God created woman as helper to man, someone to stand alongside him, but why specifically the rib? According to the Medical Art Library, "The rib cage has three important functions: protection, support and respiration. It encloses and protects the heart and lungs. It provides a strong framework onto which the muscles of the shoulder girdle, chest, upper abdomen and back can attach. It is flexible and can expand and contract by the action of the muscles of respiration."

Don't you think that God, the Great Physician, knew this when he decided to make Eve from the rib of Adam?

Above all else guard your heart, [keep and guard your heart with all vigilance [and diligence] and above all that you guard] for it is the wellspring of life. (Proverbs 4:23) Other versions phrase this scripture in different ways: *...for it affects everything you do* or *for everything you do flows from it* or, my personal favourite *for from it flows the issues of life.*

Your heart is the source of everything in your life. Your heart overflows into thoughts, your thoughts into your words, and your words into your actions. Proverbs, chapter 23, verse 7 says, *As a man thinketh in his heart, so is he.*

Now it's pretty clear from verses 24-27 of Proverbs 4 that guarding your heart is a personal thing and the writer does give some clear tips on how to do so:

Keep your mouth free from perversity; keep corrupt talk from your lips. Let your eyes look straight ahead; fix your gaze directly before you. Give careful thought to the paths of your feet and be steadfast in all your ways. Do not turn to the right or to the left; keep your foot from evil

Blatantly put, it is saying just mind your own business. But what is your business and where does Eve or 'wife' come into play?

THE FIRST FUNCTION OF EVE AS THE LIVING RIB: TO PROTECT HER OWN HEART.

This means she is to keep and guard her heart with all vigilance [and diligence] above all that she guards.

You are not Eve – untainted, unused, undefiled, unbroken Eve. You are just like me. You may feel depressed, deflated, dejected, defiled, defeated, despondent, defrauded, demoralized, and even deemed unworthy. You may have been abused, used, lied to, betrayed, raped, neglected, abandoned, rejected.

Or you may just have had your garden-variety heartbreak by some boy, who doesn't even know that he left you scared, or dented, or damaged. After all, we are taught that our first love exists to break our hearts and prepare us for 'real life'. Whatever you have been through that has weathered you, and closed you off a bit, or made you the slightest bit cynical, or cautious and untrusting, you need to heal from that.

THE FIRST PHASE OF PROTECTION AS A LIVING RIB IN GUARDING YOUR HEART IS TO HEAL.

Part of guarding your heart is to heal. It is to mend and bring your heart as close as possible to the place it was at first. This means taking inventory of what is in there, and removing everything that is not of God.

Get rid of all bitterness, rage and anger, brawling [and clamour] and slander, along with every form of malice... (Ephesians 4:31) and *but now, put away and rid yourselves [completely] of all these things: anger, rage, bad feeling toward others, curses and slander, and foul mouthed abuse and shameful utterances from your lips.*

Healing is your responsibility.

Whoever hurt you and however they hurt you is their wrongdoing; it's THEIR sin. If you are not actively taking steps toward healing and not actively seeking wholeness you are perpetuating that wrongdoing, and that is YOUR sin.

Too often we use what others have done to us, as a crutch not to love as we are supposed to, or as an excuse not to move forward, and to be a grouch. Too often we hold onto being damaged. It's our ultimate excuse for why we can never truly be happy and why we reserve the right to hurt others. But just in case no-one told you, hurting John because Peter hurt you, doesn't punish Peter by virtue of the fact that they are both males. No, it just sets you on a course for more hurt, because no matter what that hurt was, and no matter your justified reasoning for it, *whatsoever a man soweth that he shall also reap.* (Galatians 6:7-9). When you wilfully hurt another because you have been hurt, you just become the same as the person you resent for hurting you.

But there is hope. You can heal.

Healing begins with **forgiveness**, letting go, and ridding yourself of bad feelings towards others. Verse 32 of Ephesians 4 says this *And become useful and helpful and kind to one another, tender-hearted (compassionate, understanding, loving hearted) forgiving one another [readily and freely] as God in Christ forgave you.*

There are three types of forgiveness at play here: God's forgiveness, the forgiveness of self and forgiving the person deemed responsible for inflicting the harm. Forgiveness of self and seeking God's forgiveness are like two partners in a dance.

I remember when I was going through my pregnancy alone and often angry at the father who abandoned us. Dealing with all sorts of shame and rejection, I had to make a choice.

I needed to decide to heal, and have my son grow in an environment that was healthy and open and clear, and good. I needed to decide to heal, so that my son didn't pass through a channel that was tainted by hurt, bitterness and unforgiveness. I needed to choose healing over vengeance, anger and vindication, which was very difficult for me, since I am justice driven. But I made the choice, and when I finally did, I had a conversation with myself that altered my pregnancy and birthing experience. This is something I recommend: outspoken inner conversations. I started off 'speaking' to my current- ex. (Currently still making me cry, and having all sorts of control of my emotions, after having exited my life and ex-communicated himself from me, thus my 'current-ex'.)

I spoke to this 'ex' through the medium of letters. Not knowing any other way to relieve myself of these words and feelings. I relayed my anger and frustration and feelings of betrayal and abandonment by writing. I would never give him the letters of course, but I saw it done in the movies and figured there must be something to it.

At first the letters were therapeutic, and I cried as I wrote them. But the more I wrote, the more they changed direction and I found myself confessing the shame I had felt for getting pregnant. Not shame for my son, or for the life that was to be born, but shame for the fact that I had known better; shame for the fact that it was my decision to have a child out of wedlock, that has now left my son uncovered; shame that my actions would deem my son illegitimate and unfit for use; shame that I had disobeyed God in my greed for this man and a family of my own.

It was when I came to these realizations that I knew I couldn't do this to my little boy. I had to forgive myself. I had to rid myself of the bad feelings toward myself.

I learnt early on that energy cannot be lost or destroyed; it can only be transferred, or transformed. I was either going to transfer this negative energy to my son and he would then be born with a deficit, or I would have to transform it into something positive. The latter seemed preferable and I felt hopeful because of the words of Joseph in Genesis 50:20: *As for you, you meant evil against me, but God meant it for good....*" I found my 'but God' and I knew that if there was a 'but God', there was still God, and if God could forgive me, I could forgive me. That was **repentance**, an essential foundation for guarding the heart, following forgiveness.

I heard the most fitting definition of repentance from a prison preacher, and it has resonated and stuck with me ever since: "… a penthouse is situated on the highest point of a building, and the prefix 're' means 'back' or to return. In essence, to re pent, means to return to the highest point..." For me, and for purposes of the heart, I believe it's taking the heart back to the highest point, to its highest authority, to get its settings reset. Letting go is a process, but it's something you can actively do. Your thoughts do not control you. You control your thoughts.

I thought of my ex and the great betrayal he and his family had inflicted and continued to inflict on my family and my son. I thought of it in some way Every. Single. Day. Every day I allowed a thought of him to enter my mind, and I meditated on it. I went where it took me and I immersed myself in the darkness of it all, coming out drenched in tears of self-pity, and peeling back and scratching at wounds I had asked God to heal.

My mother, the wisest woman I know, saw me battle everyday with the torment of what was, and what could be, if only he would... She sat me down and told me to start monitoring my thoughts, to start tracing their origins, to see where they came from and where they were leading, and then most importantly, to STOP thinking it – to change my mind. I did have the ability after all, to change my mind and think of something else, anything else.

It took a lot of effort to do this, because the first hundred times or so, I was swallowed up by my thoughts and I just ran with them, and then only when I was in a puddle of tears, did I remember to stop. Even then, I seemed to find a pleasure in the pain. I practised letting go as often as I could remember to do it, until it got to a point that I literally cut myself off in the middle of a thought like "Girl! We don't have time for this. Moving right along."

My point is that, just as in Ephesians 5:27, where the bride of Christ is presented to Himself without spot or blemish, so we must prepare to present ourselves that way as a bride, taking on the official form of a wife. In fact, Revelation 19:7 states that *...for the marriage of the Lamb [at last] has come and His Bride has prepared herself...* Now I know that Paul in Ephesians speaks of Christ, as the husband, giving himself up for the church, and sanctifying her, having cleansed her, by the washing of the water, with the word, but Christ still looks at the heart, He always has (1 Samuel 16:7), and it is still our responsibility to prepare ourselves.

This would seem like a no-brainer, but by not healing from our hurts, whether perceived or real, whether colossal or minute, we are placing the sins and wrongs of others onto an ordinary man and asking him to be Jesus, setting ourselves up for idolatry, and setting him up for failure. Only one man took the sins of others, the sins of the world. Only one man willingly took to the cross and was crucified so that we wouldn't be. It's cruel and blasphemous for this new person to seek redemption for a past he had no part in, to be punished for something that reminds you of something that should be long gone.

When you actively seek healing, you are literally restoring your heart to its factory settings – a beautiful place to be and a magnificent thing to have – a new beginning. Too many of us have been taught that our heart's hurts, those things such as break ups, and boyfriend betrayals and the like are just part of life and shouldn't be taken so seriously. They are part of life, yes, but acting like those wounds will heal themselves is a disservice to you and to the person you should be becoming. To think those hurts haven't altered you is naïve. What's even more preposterous is the notion that only the mature hurt; that if you are 16 and have your heart broken, it doesn't mean as much to God as when you are thirty or when you are married. God cares. He's always cared. Do you have an 'ex' situation, 'ex' person, 'ex' thing, still wreaking havoc in your current, because your mind or your heart refuses to let go? Seek healing. Transfer that energy to God and allow Him to transform your heart so that you don't project another's mistakes or evils onto the unsuspecting.

How do I actively seek healing?

We tend to believe that healing is somehow our right, and we would not be wrong in thinking so, but every right has a responsibility. Our responsibility in seeking healing for our hearts and emotions is the same as when we have been physically injured. Let's say that you had your leg severely injured, to the point that the bone was beginning to show. One of the first things that you need to do is stop the bleeding. Bleeding means loss of blood.

Blood delivers necessary substances such as nutrients and oxygen to the cells and transports metabolic waste products away from those same cells. So for the purpose of this exercise, you need to stop the good from leaving your heart, and prevent waste and contaminating agents from reaching your heart. Secondly you need to make your way to a doctor, or first aid administrator. This is the repentance – going back to God, the one who heals. The third step is letting go... letting God clean the wound. And lastly, rehabilitation.

This is part of the process of guarding your heart. It is usually during this time that we offer God our advice on what we think we need. "God, just wrap a bandage around it; you can't fix it completely because I need to show [perpetrators name] exactly how he/she hurt me"

For Full restorative healing to occur, we need to go through all four steps. Let's unpack them for a better understanding:

Stopping the bleeding

Some people stop at the very first step, choosing not to stop the bleeding or bind up the wound. They choose to hold onto the hurt. Not only do they hold onto the hurt, but they project that hurt onto anyone and anything that even vaguely resembles what hurt them. They bleed their pain and subsequent insecurity on anyone daring to come close. These people never heal. In fact their wounds become septic with bitterness, and that part of them becomes totally useless, giving off the foul odour of blame, resentment and unforgiveness.

Then there are those who acknowledge their need for God to help them, but that's as far as they go – choosing to let God do his work, but only partially so – stopping at the second step.

Getting to the Physician

After cleaning the wound and stitching it up, many constantly unwrap it to see the extent of the damage, and to show others. Always touching it, having pleasure senses awoken by the sensation of the pain experienced when it is touched. They need to have access to the lesion, firstly to validate the reason for the pain they feel, and secondly as a means of holding the perpetrator captive in guilt – keeping them perpetually responsible. This is not as far-fetched as it sounds. Many hold onto trauma, in the hope that the offender would turn around or come back or even try to fix things. They believe that if the offender sees them in the pain, they would feel something whether it be remorse or pity – anything that brings them back. Phil Collins stated it beautifully when he sang "I wish I could make you turn around, turn around and see me cry; there's so much I need to say to you, so many reasons why..."

These people are so hurt, but see the wrongdoer as the only person able to fix it or make it right. Therefore going to God is just a numbing agent while they wait in vain for the wrongdoer to be the hero. It's these kinds of people who find it hard to get over things or move past relationships. They get stuck in the injury, replaying it over and over again. They take much longer to heal with new complications arising because of the exposure to bacteria. This exposure occurs to the heart, when we replay the injury over and over again, being perpetually hurt by it; we talk about the injury to anyone who wants to hear, and indulge in the opinions offered that feed the fire of anger, fear and self-pity.

Letting go

The third step is where we let GOD do all He needs to do. This part right here is one of the hardest parts of the healing process. It requires trusting God – trusting Him to re-break the bone, or to add steal pins, or to put it in a cast – however He sees fit.

I am reminded of a poem I learnt as an 8 year old girl that has never left me. I don't even know where I learnt it or why I chose to memorize it, but Connie Merrit's words explains this third step exactly.

As children bring their broken toys with tears for us to mend, I brought my broken dreams to God, because He was my friend. But, then, instead of leaving Him in peace to work alone, I hung around and tried to help, with ways that were my own. At last I snatched them back and cried, "How can you be so slow?"

"My child," He said, "What could I do? You never did let go."

Letting go here means trusting God – trusting through the pain, and not turning to your own devices to try and speed up the process (Proverbs 3:5). It involves knowing that, even though it still hurts, pain is part of the healing process. It is here that we learn the value of the sacrifice of praise.

Through Jesus, therefore let us continually offer to God a sacrifice of praise – the fruit of lips that openly profess His name. (Hebrews 13:5) A sacrifice of praise, in this instance, means praising despite the pain; it's thanking God for healing the brokenness even when we still feel broken; it's choosing to wait and worship when we would rather snatch it back and try to fix it ourselves.

The Spirit of the Sovereign LORD is on me, because the LORD has anointed me to proclaim good news to the poor. He has sent me to bind up the broken-hearted, to proclaim freedom for the captives and release from darkness for the prisoners, to proclaim the year of the LORD's favour and the day of vengeance of our God, to comfort all who mourn, and provide for those who grieve in Zion to bestow on them a crown of beauty instead of ashes, the oil of joy instead of mourning, and a garment of praise instead of a spirit of despair. They will be called oaks of righteousness, a planting of the LORD for the display of his splendour. (Isaiah 61:1-3)

Now the wound is stitched up, covered, and the open skin and bone are healing nicely. Many have allowed enough time off the leg to let it recoup, but that's where they stop, thinking that because they no longer feel the pain, that everything is okay. They just walk around with an obscure, unnatural limp, or, they never walk again. The danger with this one is that, although, they impute guilt to no-one, they have let go of the bitterness, and they don't even ever talk of the wound and the scar left by it, they live in fear. Fear of putting pressure on the leg, fear of hurting like that again. These people make it seem like walking this way, or not walking at all, is normal. So much so that those who come from them and after them, walk with a limp as well, never really knowing why, or even that they don't have to. Such people often make inward vows never to try again. They never enter the last phase.

Rehabilitation

They *will rebuild the ancient ruins and restore the places long devastated;* **they** *will renew the ruined cities that have been devastated for generations.* (Isaiah 61:4)

Rehabilitation is the act of restoring someone to health or normal life through training and therapy. This therapy is intended to help the person feel better and grow stronger; to have their strength renewed. And this therapy, like all therapy, is something that has to be done personally. It's not something that anyone else can do for you, and it's not even something that God will do for you

They that wait upon the Lord, shall renew their strength.

(Isaiah 40:31)

Waiting on the Lord is not passive inactivity, it's quite the opposite. It's Godly robust activity. Think of the work of a waiter/ waitress:

Firstly, their job is to wait on patrons. Waiters are often referred to as 'servers' – what a fitting description! A waiter, waitress or server is the liaison between the kitchen and the customer. Let's imagine, for a moment, that the kitchen is the throne room of God and that the customers are the church and unsaved. No. The server is not the middle man between God and man, rather an intercessor, a gap- stander, a repairer of the breach.

Some of you will rebuild the deserted ruins of your cities. Then you will be known as a rebuilder of walls and a restorer of homes. (Isaiah 58:12 NLT)

Yes, some of you will serve in capacities that provide healing to families and individuals, by what you have been through (your testimony). Some of you will be intercessors. An intercessor is a person who intervenes on behalf of another, by means of intercessory prayer. This takes place in the spiritual realm where the battles for our own lives, our families, our friends and our nation are won or lost.

Secondly, the waiters are the face of the restaurant.

This means that by all means they ought to practice the Optimists Creed:

Promise Yourself...

To be so strong that nothing can disturb your peace of mind. To talk health, happiness, and prosperity to every person you meet.

To make all your friends feel that there is something in them. To look at the sunny side of everything and make your optimism come true.

To think only of the best, to work only for the best, and to expect only the best.

To be just as enthusiastic about the success of others as you are about your own.

To forget the mistakes of the past and press on to the greater achievements of the future.

To wear a cheerful countenance at all times and give every living creature you meet a smile.

To give so much time to the improvement of yourself that you have no time to criticize others.

To be too large for worry, too noble for anger, too strong for fear, and too happy to permit the presence of trouble.

All this is saying, is what my mom has always said to me "Don't wear your feelings on your face." When someone has hurt or upset you, you don't punish others by being short or angry with them. You smile. You smile at strangers because you don't know who may need it. You smile because it shows love in your heart. You smile because yours may be the first face of Christ they encounter, so make it a good one.

Thirdly, and most obviously, waiters are servers. They are servants. In a restaurant scenario, the server is responsible for welcoming customers, being a menu expert, preparing and clearing tables, taking orders, stocking service areas during down times, and towards the end of the night. Servers may be tasked with menial cleaning tasks such as sweeping, mopping, taking out the trash, even cleaning the restrooms. They are to present themselves well and abide by proper grooming and appearance standards, and are required to be flexible with their times but still dependable in fulfilling all their tasks:

Welcoming customers

This applies to how we represent the gospel – how we are ambassadors of Christ. It's about passively practising The Great Commission – welcoming people into the family of believers, not as guests and one time visitors, but as members of the family.

Therefore, we are ambassadors for Christ, as though God were making an appeal through us; we beg you on behalf of Christ, be reconciled to God. (2 Corinthians 5:20)

Being a menu expert: studying the Word
I charge you in the presence of God and of Christ Jesus, who will judge the living and the dead, and in view of His appearing and His kingdom: Preach the word; be prepared in season and out of season; reprove, rebuke, and encourage with every form of patient instruction. (2 Timothy 4:1-2)

In order to speak a menu, you need to know the menu. The same applies to the Word of God. We need to spend time purposefully studying the Word that we may be able to *rightly divide the word of truth*. (2 Timothy 2:15)

Taking orders: being teachable

For whoever has [a teachable heart], to him more [understanding] will be given; and whoever does not have [a yearning for truth], even what he has will be taken away from him. (Mark 4:25 AMP)

Give instruction to a wise man, and he will be still wiser; teach a righteous man, and he will increase in learning. (Proverbs 9:9 ESV) Wisdom begets wisdom. The more time spent in the Word, the more God will reveal to you the hidden treasures.

Down time: self-preparation/ examination

We need to spend time alone with God, not just in the setting of the gathering of the saints. We need to do this to be prepared at all times to give an answer. When we are prepared, it rules out the agitation of not knowing and thus making a mockery of the cross of Christ.

But in your hearts revere Christ as Lord. Always be prepared to give an answer to everyone who asks you to give the reason for the hope that you have. But do this with gentleness and respect... (1 Peter 3:15)

Menial tasks: humility

The greatest among you shall be your servant. For whoever exalts himself will be humbled, and whoever humbles himself will be exalted. (Matthew 23:11-12) We tend to quote this scripture as saying that if you are the servant, you are the greatest among your peers, but that's misquoted because it's devoid of heart. This is one of those things we look at as though it only applied periodically, as the need arises, as though there were opportunities that presented themselves that we could show ourselves as humble, when in fact what God is addressing here is not how humble we can be, but is testing the level of the presence of pride. God hates pride.

There are six things that the Lord hates, seven that are an abomination to Him... (Proverbs 6:16)

Solomon starts this dissertation with *haughty eyes*/pride – one of the seven deadly sins. Pride is such a great abomination to God because it is a declaration of independence from Him. It was pride that caused Lucifer to think he could stand toe to toe with God. To put into perspective the depravity of pride C. S. Lewis wrote, "According to Christian teachers, the essential vice, the utmost evil, is pride. Unchastity, anger, greed, drunkenness, and all that are mere fleabites in comparison; it was through Pride that the devil became the devil: Pride leads to every other vice: it is the complete Anti-God state of mind." The biggest problem with pride is that it is one of those sins so easy to see and recognize in others yet so hard to identify in yourself. Pride stops us from helping, and from being a help. Pride stops us from learning and being open to new understanding. Pride makes us think we know stuff that we really don't and can therefore lead others astray.

Humility is the cure for pride. It means humbling yourself before God and accepting that His rule and will for your life is far better than any of your own designs. Humility is not weakness or being less than. All it is is meekness, and meekness – not weakness – is power under control. Brenda Cannon Henley writes "Meek has been a difficult root word to translate and garner all of its meaning, and it means more than we generally assign to it. Biblical meekness is not weakness but rather refers to exercising God's strength under His control — i.e. demonstrating power without undue harshness. We find in study that the English word 'meek' often lacks this blend

— of gentleness and strength that is fully needed to convey its merit."

Presenting yourself well and abiding by proper grooming and appearance standards: good spirit and ambassadors of Christ.

This is not so much how you look, or what clothes you wear, although it does have an element of that, but it's mainly about how you present yourself. It's your attitude, your demeanour, always remembering that you are an ambassador of Christ. Spiritually speaking, the apostle Paul says that is what we are when we are in Christ: *We are ambassadors for Christ, as though God were making an appeal through us; we beg you on behalf of Christ, be reconciled to God.* (2 Corinthians 5:20). No matter who we are or where we find ourselves, single or married or complicated, we need to adhere to our Great Commission. Our conduct should reflect who we are and whose we are, in our speech, in our dress, in our interactions, so that many will *be reconciled to God.* So, while inwardly we imitate Christ, outwardly we reflect Christ. I give thumbs up to our 'slaying sisters', going out there looking like their best selves – hair done, nails done, eyebrows all sleek, and there is nothing wrong with that. Nothing wrong with makeup and weaves, and dressing beautifully, but let us remember that we are the physical presence of God on earth, and the Bible requires of us to dress modestly, not boringly, but modestly. In a way that honours who we are, what we seek and Who we represent.

The Big Brother Principle.

I first heard of the Big Brother Principle in 2005 when I was attending a church service in the United States. My then pastor, Pastor Dennis Rouse of Victory World Church in Atlanta, was speaking about our conduct and behaviour as Ambassadors of Christ. He began by speaking about wine. Now I know that the drinking of wine is a very divisive topic in churches. In fact, I remember being taught the scripture in Ephesians 5:18 where it says, *Do not get drunk with wine which only leads to ruin. Instead be filled with the Holy Spirit.*" I giggle as I quote this, because it was drilled into us as part of a scripture reading when I was about 18 years old working at a primary school, and this is the part I remember most. I have been, since then, neither for nor against it, but there are many great Christians, who genuinely love Jesus and are filling the kingdom of heaven with souls, who will occasionally enjoy a glass of wine with a meal. Does this mean that they are going to hell? I think not.

But the fact of the matter is, that there are younger Christians out there, not yet secure in their walk, and who may be coming from a life of drinking and partying etc. who don't have the capacity to differentiate between their old life and this new life. People who might see a pastor having a glass of wine with his wife and wonder what is different about this new life, and wonder whether they are allowed to continue with the old? Similarly, there are those unchurched who might look at it as well, and not choose conversion because they believe the church to be a bunch of hypocrites because 'the pastor drinks.'

While Pastor Rouse did propose drinking in moderation, citing that red wine has a few benefits to the health, particularly that of heart health, he also, to the shock and horror of a few, myself included, stated that he would often enjoy a glass with a meal on his resting days. Did he feel like less of a Christian? No. Was he going to stop? No. (Shock! Horror! Gasp!) But what he did do was state the following. We should not openly do things that others have not gained victory over. Because of the wine debate, he would still enjoy his wine, but only in the privacy of his home, and in moderation. He would not expose that to those not mature enough, and would not do anything to cause another to stumble. Pastor Rouse did not believe he was sinning. He was led by his own personal relationship with God.

That's the Big Brother Principle. Protecting the younger. Making sure that you clear the path for them in way that there are few things for them to stumble over, whether it be our conduct, our dress, or our preferences. Matthew 18:6 says, *But if you cause one of these little ones who trusts in me to fall into sin, it would be better for you to have a large millstone tied around your neck and be drowned in the depths of the sea.* These little ones, these young believers, these immature believers – do not cause them to stumble. Help them along this way.

Your personal convictions [on such matters]—exercise [them] as in God's presence, keeping them to yourself [striving only to know the truth and obey His will]. Blessed (happy, to be envied) is he who has no reason to judge himself for what he approves [who does not convict himself by what he chooses to do].

But the man who has doubts (misgivings, an uneasy conscience) about eating, and then eats [perhaps because of you], stands condemned [before God], because he is not true to his convictions and he does not act from faith. For whatever does not originate and proceed from faith is sin [whatever is done without a conviction of its approval by God is sinful].

Romans 14:22-23 (AMPC)

Although this passage speaks to personal convictions, it does not give permission to you as a Christian to go out and willy nilly do things regarded as sin, because you do not feel convicted that they are wrong. Let your relationship with God lead you.

Everything we just discussed is part of rehabilitation, and all of this rehabilitation/serving is testing out your new heart; taking it for a spin; stretching it and bending it; putting pressure on it and exercising it, until all traces of injury are sufficiently worked out, and you can once again love like you've never been hurt.

The second phase of protection as a living rib is to protect the heart of the husband

Proverbs 31:11 [Study Bible] *The heart of her husband [safely] trusts her, and he will lack nothing of value [she will greatly enrich his life].*

Proverbs 31:12 [AMP] *She comforts, encourages and does him only good as long as there is life within her.*

I had always believed that it was incumbent upon partners to be each other's keepers. Secret keepers that is.

Above all, love one another deeply because love covers a multitude of sins. (1 Peter 4:8) and *Whoever covers an offense seeks love, but he who repeats a matter separates close friends.* (Proverbs 17: 9)

This point hits very close to home for me. I was in a relationship with a man I loved dearly. I would have done anything and everything for him. During those initial months and weeks, getting to know one another, and falling in love, we spoke of our dreams and our fears, we spoke of our hopes and our failures, and we confided in one another the deepest, darkest parts of ourselves. Not only the evils done to us, but also the atrocities that had come from our hand and our doing. We exposed our shame in a place we thought was 'safe'. As time passed, and things happened, as they do in relationships, I became frustrated with his shame and how it affected me and my heart, and what it was doing to our relationship, and I made the decision to expose his disgrace to his parents, under the guise of 'getting him help' and so that we could 'pray for him'. My intentions at the time, felt right, but I was coming from a place of hurt. Added to that, because of my past and my personality I am a woman with a very strong justice indicator, meaning that, in hindsight, I was really just doing it for vindication, for agreement. I wanted someone to agree with me that his shame was indeed shameful and disgraceful, and that I was justified. Needless to say, although he did all to forgive me and work past it, our relationship was never the same again. Trust is a very fragile thing, and because my trust was previously broken, I broke his, and in turn broke the inner mechanism that kept things ticking along.

Hurt people hurt people. In the words of my ex-husband, "You cannot give what you don't have" but what is more dangerous is to distribute to others what is lurking on the inside.

A man who can't lay his head on his wife's breast and find peace, comfort, and safety is a man who will begin looking for it elsewhere.

It is not sex or good cooking that keeps a man, it's not even the thought of the children brought forth in the union; what keeps a man is peace. Man's first encounter with himself and his own existence was in the Garden called Eden, where he communed with God. They walked and they talked, and he encountered the sweet, calming presence of God – the peace that surpasses all understanding. Then along came Eve, and her presence brought the serpent, and with that, a new life of toil and hardship, and I believe it has been since this moment that man has been yearning for that peace, and that sweetness that he first encountered in the Garden, that spiritual peace that was realized in and through Christ – freedom from fears, agitating passions, and moral conflicts. Man's separation from God left him to seek this lost peace from the closest thing he had to the likeness of God – Eve.

Satan foresaw this and devised a twofold plan. Firstly to use his initial weapon, doubt and mistrust, and secondly, to bring contention into the heart of wife, thus separating her further from the closest thing she had to the likeness of God, and breaking down the marriage from inside. The further he took the wife from the likeness of Christ, and the further he took the man from the likeness of God, the more likely they would be to forget Him, allow sin and substitutes to run rampant, and abdicate their God-given roles so that they would become redundant and easily replaceable. They would then basically have no need of each other. This would render them useless.

Becoming a wife means coming back to being the likeness of God.

*"And have clothed yourselves with the new [spiritual self], which is [ever in the process of being] renewed and remolded into [fuller and more perfect knowledge upon] knowledge **after the image (the likeness) of Him Who created it.***

Clothe yourselves therefore, as God's own chosen ones (His own picked representatives), [who are] purified and holy and well-beloved [by God Himself, by putting on behavior marked by] tenderhearted pity and mercy, kind feeling, a lowly opinion of yourselves, gentle ways, [and] patience [which is tireless and long-suffering, and has the power to endure whatever comes, with good temper].

Be gentle and forbearing with one another and, if one has a difference (a grievance or complaint) against another, readily pardoning each other; even as the Lord has [freely] forgiven you, so must you also [forgive].

And above all these [put on] love and enfold yourselves with the bond of perfectness [which binds everything together completely in ideal harmony].

And let the peace (soul harmony which comes) from Christ rule (act as umpire continually) in your hearts [deciding and settling with finality all questions that arise in your minds, in that peaceful state] to which as [members of Christ's] one body you were also called [to live]. And be thankful (appreciative), [giving praise to God always].

Let the word [spoken by] Christ (the Messiah) have its home [in your hearts and minds] and dwell in you in [all its] richness, as you teach and admonish and train one another in all insight and intelligence and wisdom [in spiritual things, and as you sing] psalms and hymns and spiritual songs, making melody to God with [His] grace in your hearts. And whatever you do [no matter what it is] in word or deed, do everything in the name of the Lord Jesus and in [dependence upon] His

Person, giving praise to God the Father through Him.

Wives, be subject to your husbands [subordinate and adapt yourselves to them], as is right and fitting and your proper duty in the Lord." (Colossians 3: 10, 12-18)

It is quite a lengthy portion of scripture, but I do believe it reinforces what I have been trying to say, and I feel that it is no coincidence that it runs straight into admonitions to the husband / wife relationship.

In preparation for your role as a wife, God requires of you to take on the qualities that were yours in the Garden. He requires you to live in your truest self and that self, contrary to much of today's teaching, is the image and likeness of Christ. It is only here, that that eluding peace that Adam has been looking for, can be obtained –

the peace that settles with finality the questions that arise, the peace that quenches the embers of doubt – Satan's primary weapon – in the water of the Word.

Paul also reinforces the notion in this portion of scripture, that we ought to do ALL in the name of the Lord, as unto God. Doesn't this resonate with our earlier statement that Eve honoured God in honouring her God-given role to Adam? Peter says it explicitly in the 1st book of Peter chapters 1 and 2, when he speaks of being born again and taking on the new self. I believe the same principles of transformation apply when one is transforming from one glory to another, whether that be in the annals of salvation or from transitioning from woman to wife.

This is being Born Again:
Acknowledgment
Repentance
Transformation
Rebirth

It's coming back to the Garden, back to your place of origin, and emerging as a new being – regenerated (born again), having taken on the very nature of God, living out the fruit of the SPIRIT. He even touches on the themes of once again being rectified and being *made fit for service, being redeemed (ransomed) from the useless (fruitless) way of living inherited by tradition from [our] forefathers* (1 Peter 1:18).

Once again we are becoming a suitable helpers. He even goes so far as to urge and implore these newly created creatures, who live as exiles in this world, to abstain from the sensual urges (the evil desires, the passions of the flesh, your lower nature) that wage war against the soul. Another version describes it as fleshly lusts.

This is also in direct correlation to the mandate of the woman seeking to be a wife: to abstain from sexual relations and advances and to keep herself morally and sexually pure, to walk circumspectly. In her old life, relationships might have naturally included sex but in this new life she flees from sexual immorality. For many woman, this is the hardest part of becoming a wife, what with all this talk of 'sexual compatibility', and the fear that if you don't agree to some heavy petting at the very least, you will be labelled a 'prude'; and what man is going to want to be with you then? Right?

Answer: The right one.

There is great hope because Peter does explain the reward of conducting yourself honourably and righteously. (1 Peter 2:12) He indicates that others might be watching / witnessing your conduct [good deeds] and come to glorify God. This, along with your new nature (kindness, love, forbearance etc.) puts you as part of the plan of redemption. It always comes back to conduct, kindness and love, and the Great Commission. *Don't you see how wonderfully kind, tolerant and patient God is with you? Does this mean nothing to you? Can't you see that His kindness is intended to turn you from your sin [turn you to repentance].* (Romans 2:4 NLT)

Safety exists in peace and kindness- transcendent peace and genuine kindness. There is no Godly peace in contention and tolerance.

The third phase of protection as the living rib is placement for protection

Under His wing.

I don't know about you, but as a woman, one of the best feelings, especially in that in-love phase is to snuggle yourself into

115

he space in his arm. You know which one? The one right under his arm.

Whether it is to lie cradled there and watch a movie, with your ear to his heart, and his arm draped over you, or to walk with him as he pulls you close and tells the world that you are his, under the covering of his arm, and your ear still at his heart. The thing is though, no matter how you look at it, you have to lower yourself to get in there. That is the place from which you were made, and that is the place you need to be, and to get back there, requires a lowering of the head, a submission of the frame. Under. Under a covering. Under a higher authority. Under Protection.

Psalm 91:4

He will spread his wings over you and keep you secure. [Contemporary English Version]

He will cover you with his wings; you will be safe in his care. [Good News Translation]

When you refuse to submit, you are refusing protection, and you are refusing to be comforted.

*O Jerusalem, Jerusalem… how often have I wanted to gather your children together as a hen protects her chicks beneath her wings, **but you would not let me.** (Matthew 23:37 NLT)*

Submission
Wives, be subject (be submissive and adapt yourselves) to your own husbands as [a service] to the LORD. (Ephesians 5:22)

For many women today, the word submission conjures up images of brutal men forcing their will upon weak women; women who have very little recourse, other than to remain residing in abusive relationships because their minds have been conditioned to 'stay'. Submission, to many of us, means abuse or being a doormat. But the reality, and in truth, is that submission is such a beautiful rewarding act of selflessness and obedience, and it's not obedience to a man. It's obedience to the will of God.

It's obedience to God Himself. Submission is not the forcefully breaking of someone's will, because no-one can force your heart to submit. Submission is an internal intentional, conscious, voluntary action and it starts on the inside with willingness. I can force you to do something, but I can't force you to be willing to do it. I can break your will down to the point where you resign to my wishes, but it still won't make you willing. Willingness is your choice; therefore submission is your choice.

The best way I ever heard submission described was in the telling of the interaction between a parent and child. This particular parent had asked her child to sit down. On the first verbal request, the child refused, causing the parent to change her tone to one of a more stern nature. This also failed.

It was at this point that the parent picked the child up and made her sit down, but all she did was get up again. The parent did this twice with the headstrong little girl, both of them blatantly putting their frustration on display in a battle of wills. Finally the mom gave her a smack on the bottom and the little girl remained seated. Physically. Her will though, was still standing. Her body had been forced to do something that her spirit did not want to do, and therefore did not do. One look at that little girl and you knew she had been overpowered but had not resolved herself to that position.

Forced submission creates anger, resentment and a rebellious spirit. Godly submission creates peace and harmony, and fosters unity; and it empowers, rather than taking power away. Submission is more of an attitude of the heart, than it is a physical action.

Godly submission is:

- Selfless

- Doesn't have an 'I don't need you' mentality, but rather acknowledges dependence.

- Is a teachable, pliable spirit:

  In like manner, you married women, be submissive to your own husbands [subordinate yourselves as being secondary to and dependent on them and adapt yourselves to them].

- (1 Peter 3:1 (a) AMPC)

- A tool for redemption in the home:

...so that even if any [husbands] do not obey the Word [of God], they may be won over not by discussion but by the [godly] lives of their wives, when they observe the pure and modest way in which you conduct yourselves, together with your reverence (submission) [for your husband; you are to feel for him all that reverence includes: to respect, defer to, revere him—to honour, esteem, appreciate, prize, and, in the human sense, to adore him, that is, to admire, praise, be devoted to, deeply love, and enjoy your husband]. (1 Peter 3:1 (b), 2 AMPC)

- Appreciation

- Enjoyment

- An outward display of inner Beauty:

Let not yours be the [merely] external adorning with [elaborate] [b] interweaving and knotting of the hair, the wearing of jewellery, or changes of clothes; but let it be the inward adorning and beauty of the hidden person of the heart, with the incorruptible and unfading charm of a gentle and peaceful spirit, which [is not anxious or wrought up, but] is very precious in the sight of God. For it was thus that the pious women of old who hoped in God were [accustomed] to beautify themselves and were submissive to their husbands [adapting themselves to them as themselves secondary and dependent upon them]. (1 Peter 3:3-5AMPC)

- Treasured by God
- Obedient

It was thus that Sarah obeyed Abraham [following his guidance and acknowledging his headship over her by] calling him lord (master, leader, authority). And you are now her true daughters if you do right and let nothing terrify you [not giving way to hysterical fears or letting anxieties unnerve you]. (1 Peter 3:6AMPC)

Godly submission provides:

- Peace
- A covering
- Comfort – Submit under his arm in that place of comfort.

One can refuse to be comforted as in Matthew 23:37. You can refuse to abide in a place of safety and comfort.

Godly submission is not something that just happens the moment you meet Mr Right. It's something you practice. It's learned behaviour. You have to adapt yourself to submission. You need to make the necessary changes and alterations until it fits in line with the God given vision.

I have heard many married women say "I would submit to him if he gave me something to submit to" or "if my husband would just do this, I can submit", but Godly submission, much like many other biblical principles, isn't subject to what someone else is or is not doing. All God requires of you is to do your part and trust Him with the rest. The most frequent and problematic excuses I have heard from woman not submitting and letting him lead, is that "I just don't trust him to lead us, I don't trust that he will make the right decision." I will let you in on a little secret my mom told me... it's not your job to trust him, it's your job to trust God with him. Just place him in the folds of God's hands in prayer and leave him there, then do what God has mandated you to do.

THE SECOND FUNCTION OF EVE AS THE LIVING RIB: SUPPORT

"...provides a strong framework onto which the muscles of the shoulder girdle, chest, upper abdomen and back can attach..."

It has often been said, that behind every successful man is a strong woman. In fact, to date, I have read many variables of this statement, from, 'is a surprised woman' to 'is a praying wife' - the latter being my favourite.

She carries him.

I have found that few things bring a person to his knees more quickly than applying weight or pressure on the shoulder. There's a certain pressure point, that if you press it at the right place, you can bring even a sizeable man to his knees.

Many think that submission is some sort of inactivity awaiting instruction, but it is not. It's the girding up of self for what lies ahead. Although this position of 'under his wing' is one of comfort and protection it can, with the slightest displacement of weight, very quickly become a position requiring fortitude. The mutuality of marriage demands a constant shifting of strengths. While these are practiced simultaneously, it's just the degree and need that changes. In other words, although a husband always covers his wife, and although she always remains under submission to his authority, it's a dance of changing steps as the need requires.

One of the benefits of the 'under his wing' position, is that, when the tables turn, when weight is shifted, you become the support; the pillar holding everything up. Even when the weight brings you to your knees, never forget that you are strongest on your knees. The paradox of the position of submission, is that, from that same position you gain leverage and power, but you gain it in heaven. Submission places you in a position of power.

Louis Sullivan once said, in relation to architecture, that "Form follows function". This quote stated that the shape of an object or its environment should be modelled based on its intended purpose. Function should dictate the design. In fact, the full quote speaks volumes in all its beauty and accuracy:

"Whether it be the sweeping eagle in his flight, or the open-apple blossom, the toiling work-horse, the blithe swan, the branching oak, the winding stream at its base, the drifting clouds, over all the coursing sun, form ever follows function, and this is the law.

Where function does not change, form does not change. The granite rocks, the ever-brooding hills, remain for ages; the lightning lives, comes into shape, and dies, in a twinkling.

It is the pervading law of all things organic and inorganic, of all things physical and metaphysical; of all things human and superhuman, of all true manifestations of the head, of the heart, of the soul, that the life is recognizable in its expression form ever follows function. This is the law."

Plainly put, how we were made, and where we are made to fit determines our function, and in this instance, our function is support. A pillar or a column in architecture is a structural element that transmits, through compression, the weight of the structure above, to other structural elements below.

So... in layman's terms, your placement 'under his wings' puts you in the perfect position to absorb the weight from the structure above – the covering, the husband – and distribute it to the other structural elements below, but the important thing to note is that there have to be other structural elements below. These elements are fundamental components such as faith, a foundation in the Word, and a habitual prayer life. These need to be found in the wife.

When we are brought to our knees that's when the enemy thinks surrender is eminent, but we know once on our knees, that's when the battle really begins. Oscar Wild said it best when he said, "Each of us is a hollow pillar. Even when you appear to be supporting the framework of your life [and business] you are not carrying the load. It is Christ Jesus. Accept this truth and find true strength."

We are girded with inner strength in the hollow places when we find ourselves deeply rooted in Christ as our foundation.

Plant your roots in Christ and let Him be the foundation of your life. Be strong in your faith just as you were taught. And be grateful. (Colossians 2:7 CEV)

In the early 90's, a group of psychologists led by Ronald Finke also concluded that function follows form; however, their basic premise was that one could create an object of any form then uncover the potential benefits of that object.

Unfortunately, that's what we are faced with today. We take a woman and tell her that she can be anything, which in and of itself is not a bad thing, but what we direct her to become is usually a feminine variation of a man. Telling her that she can have it all. She can be the pursuer and the protector and the head of her home. But the disclaimer in fine print, is that she usurps the role previously held by her male counterpart, and she loses the soft quality of being a woman.

This version of the law that function follows form, can lead to chaos and abnormal use. It leads to identity crises, and dilemmas about sexual identity. It has led to the woman becoming the man, men remaining children, and children trying to be adults, and in all this the woman is a mythical creature that once existed before she left her throne to explore other roles.

The role of attachment

"...provides a strong framework onto which the muscles of the shoulder girdle, chest, upper abdomen and back can attach..." This attachment of the shoulder girdle, chest, upper abdomen and back is of great significance. The function of the chest muscle is to provide protection to vital organs, not just the heart, but the lungs and liver and major vessels as well, and to provide stability of movement to the shoulder girdle. The function of the shoulder girdle is to give strength and range of motion to the arm. Fittingly so, the back muscles are soft tissue around the spine that plays a key role in the health of the back. These muscles allow one to stand, and lift heavy objects.

Let's break this down.

Your husband's attachment to you affords him not only the protection of his heart, but also of his dreams, his hopes, and his aspirations – the things that drive him and motivate him. Not only does she protect those by not ridiculing them and by believing in him, but that protection and belief provides him with the surety, stability,

and focus needed to accomplish them; added to that, it also provides strength of character through his confidence that he is capable of a wider range of success, a wider scope of influence, and a motion of the arm that allows him to reach out and help others.

She is the soft tissue around the bones of ideas that allows him to stand tall, to walk straight and circumspectly. She is the boost he needs to lift the heavy objects that would otherwise just be an insurmountable obstacle. Without the wife pulling together and making a place for him to attach, he will never be all that he needs to be – all that is inside him to be.

Yes, behind every truly successful man, is a praying wife.

THE THIRD FUNCTION OF EVE
AS THE LIVING RIB: RESPIRATION

"…It is flexible and can expand and contract by the action of the muscles of respiration."

Respiration is the action of breathing: this is the process of moving air into and out of the lungs to facilitate gas exchange with the internal environment, mostly by bringing in oxygen and flushing out carbon dioxide. (Wikipedia) Basically, respiration is taking in from the environment in which we find ourselves those things we need for survival, keeping the good and discarding the bad. A good wife is an irreplaceable key to a husband's ability to do this – to differentiate between a good idea, and a God idea. She is a sounding board that gives life to his vision by breathing into it her input, her guidance, and her wisdom derived from the process of prayer.

Breathing is subconscious, it doesn't stop when we are asleep; even so the wife is breathing into dreams that lie dormant, and into a vision that has fallen asleep, often performing CPR to awaken the dreamer, to arise the sleeper. ...*Awake O sleeper, and arise from the dead, and Christ will shine on you.* (Ephesians 5:14)

Breathing requires flexibility of the rib. 'Flexible' means capable of bending [easily] without breaking.

We are hard pressed on every side, but not crushed; perplexed but not in despair, persecuted but not abandoned; struck down but not destroyed. (2 Corinthians 4:8-9 NIV) This kind of flexibility speaks of fortitude – the emotional power or reserves and the ability to withstand adversity. Fortitude comes from the Latin word *fortitudo* meaning 'strength'.

This is the strength to keep believing when the odds are against you; the strength to keep fighting when it seems that the battle is lost; the strength to keep trusting when God seems silent; the strength to keep praying when words fail you; the strength to carry your husband when the weight has shifted. It is the courage and bravery when dealing with pain or difficulty over a prolonged period. Everyone can be strong for a while; everyone can believe for a while. Any woman can stand by a man through difficulty for a while, and encourage him for a while, and honour him for a while through hardship and failure, but only a wife can do it for as long as it's required, like a rib, expanding and contracting as the situation requires, until relief is provided.

Marriage is demanding. It demands effort and intention. Like a toddler, it cannot be left to its own devices; it needs guidance and it needs to be fed and cleaned and disciplined and loved. You need to love, not only your spouse, but your marriage as well. You need to nurture this entity, and help it grow as you grow.

I am reminded of the Tyler Perry movie *Acrimony*. I don't want to get into the debate of who was right and who was wrong, and if she was crazy or justified, but I do want to draw your attention to a few things that I gained from the movie.

While watching *Acrimony*, I couldn't help but wonder what this couple's scenario would have been had they known Jesus. Would Melinda have been able to bear up under him as he searched to fill the hunger created by his need for success – his need to prove that what he had in him was indeed something worthwhile and able to change and improve lives, including theirs?

With my limited interpretation, the only thing wrong with this marriage was time. Time was playing against them. They had let time run on and didn't once stop to nurture the marriage. The individuals in this union were no longer in unity, they were a cat and dog tied at the tail and thrown over a washing line. Think about it. Had she waited with him, believed a little longer, had a little more faith for a few more months, the entire movie would not exist. But she had no more in her, because it had taken too much time and he still had not succeeded.

Unfortunately, when God gives a man a vision, he rarely gives him a timeline. Joseph waited 13 years, Abraham, God's friend, waited 25 years, Moses waited 40 years, and even though David was anointed as king, it took him 15 years before he actually ascended the throne. Even Jesus waited 30 years.

Let's imagine for one minute that God had given Robert a vision; that God had called and spoken to him about all the things he spoke to Melinda about. The boat, the house, the travels... they were all in Robert, God had placed them there, and here comes Melinda, our very own Vashti.

She believes in him. For a while.

She stands with him. For a while.

She undertakes his dream. For a while.

But she never really invests herself. She invests her time in doing the things she believes he has failed to do as a man, so she usurps his role. But she doesn't invest that time in him, or in his calling. So she becomes stagnant, then bitter, and then kills the marriage, and with that, leaves her throne open for a new queen. Yet the dream is still inside Robert. What God has called him to, is still inside him.

Pay attention here to Esther 4:14 – *If you keep quiet at a time like this, deliverance and relief for the Jews will arise from some other place, but you and your relatives will die. Who knows if perhaps you were made queen for just such a time as this?*

Were you made queen, for such a time as this? To awaken the sleeping king? Or to speak life into that dream, and resuscitate it?

So shall My word be that goes forth from My mouth; It shall not return to Me void, But it shall accomplish what I please, And it shall prosper in the thing for which I sent it. (Isaiah 55:11)

The word, the dream, the vision WILL be accomplished, even if a new queen has to be raised up to fulfill it.

So let's not get tired of doing what is good. At just the right time we will reap a harvest of blessing if we don't give up. (Galatians 6:9) In the age in which we live, everything is instant and gratification is immediate, and we ask, "Can she really be expected to wait so long? To sacrifice so long?" The answer is yes. Obedience is the expectation. Had Melinda and Robert known their God, and honoured their roles, and trusted in Him, their marriage would not have been sacrificed, because communion with God would have kept them holding on to what they had hoped for, the thing she could not see. We are often told of Abraham, who is the Father of Faith, the one who *against all hope, in hope believed* (Romans 4:18), but we forget to see faith as a partnership in marriage.

For Abraham to indeed become the father of many nations, his partnership with Sarah was vital. He tried having a baby with Hagar, but this proved not only futile to the promise, but also problematic to the union. It was the child born of both Abraham **and** Sarah that was the beginning of the fulfilment of the promise. Yes, Sarah did initially laugh at the promise given, but she bought into it. In fact, she became so invested in the promise God made to Abraham, her husband, that she tried to fulfil it herself. His faith became her faith.

She began seeing what he saw. I imagine she began preparing for it: making the tent child-friendly and knitting booties and bonnets. She became so excited for it that the excitement eventually turned into impatience, which led to the whole Hagar debacle. But the point here is how invested Sarah became in her husband's promise, his vision, his dream.

Fortitude is faith in action. It's waiting and trusting God to do what He said He would do. Faith, in marriage, is a partnership. The two have become one, and should work as one engine... two wheels on the same axel, driving the vehicle in the same direction. In the unforgettable words of John Hagee, from his book *What Every Woman Wants in a Man/ What Every Man Wants in a Woman* when you come before God, "...God sees both of you or he sees neither of you"

Breathe life into the God-given dreams of your husband, pray life into his ideas, give his promise wings with encouragement, and emotional, spiritual and prayerful investment. He may lose hope, he may become discouraged, he may want to forget and say "Did God really say?" but you need to develop the fortitude in faith that, against ALL hope, in hope, believes.

Two people are better than one, for they can help each other succeed. If one falls his friend can help him up. But pity the man who falls and has no one to help him up. Also if two lie down together, they will keep warm. But how can one keep warm alone? Though one may be overpowered two can defend themselves. A cord of three strands is not quickly broken. (Ecclesiastes 4:9-12)

Your Husband, you, and God – the Triune God. How can this be broken at all?

Chapter 9
FIND

A wife is not something that is flaunted or put on display. It is something that needs to be sought after, searched for in secret places. A wife is a hidden treasure that must be unearthed.

Men are hunters. Men are warriors. Men are chasers. Women were not designed for the chase. We were designed to be receptors and responders.

I found a quote online by Patti Stanger from her series *The Millionaire Matchmaker* which states, quite poetically "Give him space, to chase. Be the Hunted." Now it doesn't take a genius to figure out what this has to do with 'Find'. Men generally tell us what we are in for. A man's behaviour will let you know the kind of relationship or connection he is offering. The problem is that women don't listen. They choose to bypass that in the hope that he will change for her, or that she can change him.

I was once in a relationship with a man who explicitly told me the thing that should have ended our relationship. Instead I saw it as a challenge. We were arguing about his lack of making a commitment by way of proposing. He would not say that he didn't want to, but he also didn't take the necessary steps to doing so. During this tense discussion, I listed every reason why I would make him a good wife, and every way in which I had proven to be an asset to him. I asked what I was doing wrong, and if there was anything more I could I do. Those were rhetorical questions to me, and I assumed they were to him to, but he responded with something I have never forgotten. He said "If a man wants to choose you, he'll choose you. If he doesn't, he won't." In his mind, he was stating that he had 'chosen me'; he was with me wasn't he? That should have been enough to keep me quiet, and in my desperation and stupidity, that day, it was enough. But what he was, in essence, telling me, was that he had no intention or desire of taking our relationship to the next level. He was happy to keep me here, as his, but never take ownership of me – never make me a permanent fixture in his life. He wanted to keep me around, but was inwardly convinced that there had to be better in store for him. But in case there wasn't, at least I was still here. He had no real reason to get rid of me. And why would he?

I saw to his every need. I cooked his favourite meals, packed him thoughtful lunches, planned (and paid for) all our vacations, entertained his friends, took a vested interest in his hobbies, to the point that they became mine! When he walked in from a long day's work there would be a glass of water waiting for him. After his shower from gym, his supper would be waiting for him on a tray with a knife, fork, and napkin all neatly set out, as well as his favourite condiments. He had his drink ready and after supper, I would make him a cup of tea just the way he liked it. I served him in every way possible. I gave him the freedom to pursue new hobbies and interests, and supported him in his work stresses. I never denied him anything, not forgetting that he had sex on tap. I wanted him to see what life would be like if we were to get married.

I am naturally a home maker and a nurturer. Those are my desires. It gives me great pleasure to do those things, and I was very proud of how I 'honoured' him. But never did I once stop to think that I was possibly sowing in the wrong place. Nor did I stop to think if I was being honoured, whether I was honouring myself, honouring my beliefs and my own worth, and most important, if I was honouring God. I was the poster child for trying to earn love and commitment. But mainly, I was providing the definition for "Why buy the cow, when you can get the milk for free?"

When I was thinking about this chapter, I asked God "What can I say about 'FIND'?" A 'lost' object has no control over being found. I thought about my previous relationship and how I had done everything and still walked away from that relationship no closer to being anyone's wife. I couldn't make him choose me, despite my best efforts.

How do I write about 'Find' – this word that has jumped out at me every single time I read that scripture (Proverbs 18:22)? I knew there had to be more to it than just hoping a man would stumble across me, or that if I sat patiently in the right places, he would notice me. The longer I remained single, the more 'find' seemed to mean putting myself out there, and going to every social and gathering that I could, in the hope that my potential husband would be there too. It even meant making sure that I was always dolled up, and dressed to the nines, even if I just wanted to pop into the Spar to buy a loaf of bread. Who knew? Maybe Mr Right would be there too, and we'd both reach for the same loaf of bread, and voila! Our own 'meet-cute'! It was exhausting. And still I was asking God: what do I write about 'Find'?

In the stillness, after a few deep breaths, Gods response to me was 'The Pearl of Great Price'. That was all I heard Him drop into my spirit. My mind immediately went to the depths of the ocean, to a little silver oyster, hidden in the trenches of the underwater world, just sitting there. My oyster just sits there, looking almost inanimate. It sits there, for days, for weeks, for months and even years, looking like nothing, blended into the background. But on the inside of it is a huge pink pearl, a magnificent pearl, a pearl that might be placed in a ring and treasured as a family heirloom from generation to generation, a pearl whose value is intrinsically known by anyone who looks at it – a priceless pearl! *A lot of good it does anyone under the sea*, I think to myself.

And that's when it hit me. Just as it's our responsibility consciously to become the wife of Proverbs 31, there's also an element of that role being drawn out of you, by the right man. Any other man will only see you as an oyster, as an aphrodisiac to his pleasures, but the right man will seek out the pearl in you. Again the Holy Spirit whispered "The Pearl of Great Price".

This now led me to Matthew 13:45-46 *Again the kingdom of heaven is like a merchant looking for fine pearls. When he found one of great value, he went away and sold everything he had and bought it.* Yes, Jesus is talking about the kingdom of heaven in this parable, but I want to draw your attention to this man. This man who was already someone seeking treasure. He wasn't looking for trinkets; he wasn't looking for pretty substitutes. He was looking for the real deal, and when he found it, he became desperate to possess it, and immediately sold all he had to buy it. He discarded everything to make room for this one thing. There was no room for anything that would compete with it for a seat at the table.

Too many of us settle for men who make us part of a collection and are only looking for pretty substitutes, or for aphrodisiac seeking men who are not interested in value, only in what looks pretty and makes them look and feel good. And because there's no value to the one collecting, as it were, they easily move on to the next shiny trinket.

Think back to when you were a child, before tablets and cell phones and computer games. We had our imaginations, and we fully utilized their deep recesses. As little girls, we would play house, carefully tending to our babies and baking mud pies, and cooking wet muddy 'meals' mixed with grass and any other 'ingredients' we could get our hands on. Boys on the other hand, played at being sword- wielding pirates, fighting off bad guys and discovering treasures hidden in deep jungles amid fierce creatures. If the girls were allowed to play along, then it was that they were being rescued by these little warrior heroes. That play, ultimately and most fundamentally, showcased boys in their natural innate role as pursuer, protector and treasure seeker.

This is their natural habitat.

This very idea conjures up mental images of stories I read or were read to me. Such stories as the boy who never grew up: *Peter Pan*, and his lost boys, always seeking out lost treasure and fighting off pirates; or *Robin Hood*, whose pursuit of gold and silver, led him onto the pursuit of a different kind of treasure – justice for the downtrodden, and ultimately Maid Marion. Or how about the numerous books written on treasure hunts, like Robert Louis Stevenson's very famous *Treasure Island*, which introduced us to the likes of Long John Silver? Which young boy hasn't, at some point in his growing up, drawn a fictitious treasure map, where X marks the spot? Or tried to find the pot of gold that lies at the end of the rainbow?

If these examples fall outside of your age bracket, why not look to the likes of the box office hit *Ready Player One*. Here the plot is also about a young man in search of treasure – a Golden Egg, but in this case, it all takes place in virtual reality. The Golden Egg grants ownership of the oasis to its finder. In the end however, treasure hunt winner, Wade Watts, wins in more ways than one, when he walks away with the heart of Samantha, his gaming companion.

Treasure.

The prospect of hidden treasure, and the pursuit to find it, has appealed to the imagination of children throughout history, regardless of race or creed. But let's get out of fiction for a minute and look at history. What led men to leave the comfort of their homes, and even countries, to live in makeshift tents, in cold, barely habitable places? Was it not the pursuit of gold or diamonds or other precious metals or gems that they deemed as treasure, as worthy of pursuit? All the gold and diamond rushes the world over had this one thing in common. Men who would do whatever it takes for however long it takes, who would sacrifice self and comfort and health, and warmth and pleasure, in the hope of obtaining a nugget of their own.

Men are fundamentally pursuers of treasure, no matter what that treasure may be. I believe it is hard wired within them to be hunters, chasers, expeditioners. Men, yes MEN, from many walks of life, and in various positions of influence have supported this theory.

Steve Harvey, well known comedian, television host, and author has long been an active global advocate for speaking into the lives of women on what men really think about love, commitment and relationships. Just on a side note: why do women think that another woman would understand the psyche of men? We keep saying "men don't speak", but when they do, we seldom listen to what they say. TD Jakes said it best, when in a sermon he commented on how women are being advised about men in magazine articles written by women for women, telling women "the nine things a man needs..." Jakes said, "Most sincerely, she don't know what she's talking about". I share that sentiment. Deeply.

Back to Steve Harvey... Harvey was quoted as saying this "Men are by nature hunters, and woman have been put in the position of being the prey."

If you are more old school, and don't quite agree with Harvey, then look at what Alfred Tennyson, poet of the 1800's had to say... "Man is the Hunter; woman is his game. The sleek and shining creatures of the chase, we hunt them for the beauty of their skins; they love us for it..." And yes we do.

So now back to the 'Find'...

Earlier I assumed that the 'lost' item has no control over being found, and that is absolutely true, assuming the item is 'lost'. I had firstly to wrap my head around the fact that I am not lost. As a single woman, as an older single woman, I am not 'lost'. Although I did feel lost and forgotten for the longest time. You see, I was once married. It wasn't a long marriage, and it wasn't a particularly healthy or happy marriage, but it was my marriage, and it gave me somewhere to belong. I had gotten married, and had changed surnames – my first public act of submission as a wife. When I got divorced, I struggled with that act. I struggled with who I was. When I got married, I traded in 'Scoble', for 'Dillon', but now being divorced, I was neither. I couldn't just go back to being my father's daughter, as one who had never left the home. And I was no longer a wife. The spiritual act that took place as my dad handed me over to my groom, on our wedding day, symbolized the transition, the crossover, from innocence into maturity, from daughter into wife, from one covering of authority and protection to another. There was no ceremony for handing me back, for once again placing me under the covering of my father. I felt uncovered, exposed, and lost. I felt like the sock that goes missing in the wash... you know it exists, you just don't know where. I felt lost in another dimension. As an older single lady, I form part of a contingent of woman who don't quite fit in anywhere. We're too old to be part of the young adult unmarrieds, and we are too single, and too much of a threat to marriages to enjoy relationships with our peers who are blessed enough to be married, or to *still* be married. Meeting people at this age and stage is difficult, because most have already formed their circle. It's complicated, because it's hard not to become desperate and risk being taken advantage of, and, it's compromising to your spirituality because how do you keep a new relationship pure when you've already bought tickets to that ride? What are you saving yourself for? Lost.

But when I decided that in Christ, I was none of those things but that I was a woman whom God is hopefully, not hopelessly, in love with, and that He is just as concerned with my happiness and heart as I am, and when I found myself and my worth in Christ, I could then only see the treasure and gem that God sees me as. When I accepted that God is forever pursuing me and that He went to great lengths to have me, and that every day He desires me, and woos me, I slowly began finding myself. I no longer saw myself as a replaceable, used, lost sock, but came to identify myself as the Pearl that God had made. So I believe that that is the place to start. Find yourself. Find yourself in Christ. He specializes in the niche market of the lonely, lost, hurting, and misplaced.

Sometimes all we see of ourselves is what we have been through, and what was said about us. But I want you to remember these three vital, unalterable facts:

1. The truth needs no defence. You never have to justify or defend who God says you are. That is what you are. Period. If God says that you are a fish, you had better believe that you are a fish. If God says you are beautiful, worthy, loved, strong, and captivating, then guess what you are? And here's the deal, it's not an 'if', it is! This is just the tip of the iceberg of what God says you are. Does God lie?

2. Whether or not you believe something, doesn't make it any less or any more true. Your belief, or lack thereof, doesn't change the fact. It determines how you walk through life, but it doesn't change the fact. If God said that you are a fish and you refuse to believe it, you will go through the waters of life struggling to breathe as you try to row yourself to your destination. Let go of the paddle and swim! Even if others don't believe, does that change the fact? I can call a cat a fish all day long, but all that cat will do is continue to find spots in the sun where she can lie, and posts to dig her nails into. That cat will never grab its tail and go running for the ocean. That cat, that cannot reason, knows who it is, and will live according to that. Shouldn't you? Don't allow people to tell you who you are. More importantly, don't allow those who have refused to love you, to tell you who you are. The fact that they wouldn't love you, or they couldn't love you, doesn't make you unlovable.

Someone else's deficiency should not become your handicap.

3. And lastly, there are no degrees of truth. There is only the truth and the lie when it comes to God. He doesn't have grey areas. He doesn't have half-truths and He doesn't have anything that He needs to repent from; no retracting of statements. Anything outside of what God has said is a LIE. Full stop. Don't let anyone convince you otherwise. Don't let life convince you that you are no longer a treasure. Yes, you may have been through the most.

Someone might have taken you and not seen your worth and used you and discarded you and left you on a dump. Or life might have put you through the wringer and buried you beneath the dirt of insecurity, self-doubt, insults and rejection, but it doesn't change who you are. I guarantee you that if anyone found a R100 note, crumpled up and dirty, probably stinking with a few questionably wet spots, in the mire of a landfill, they wouldn't leave it there. They would pick it up, wipe it off and take it home to fill a need. The R100 note never stopped being a R100 note in the landfill. It just went through a couple of things.

Once you have found yourself, you need to understand your worth. You need to believe what God says. One way of doing this is taking the time to research what the Bible says about you, then taking the time to listen to what the voice of God says about you.

After listening and receiving, you need to start speaking and, most importantly, you have to start ACTING LIKE YOU BELIEVE IT.

But we have this treasure in jars of clay, to show that the surpassing power belongs to God and not to us. We are afflicted in every way, but not crushed; perplexed, but not driven to despair; persecuted, but not forsaken; struck down, but not destroyed; (2 Corinthians 4:7-9 (ESV) and *Since we have the same spirit of faith according to what has been written, I believed, and so I spoke, we also believe, and so we also speak…* (2 Corinthians 4:13 ESV)

I know that it's hard to believe that God has made you to be a wife, when everyone around you is already married; it's hard to believe that you are 'wife material', or that you have the highest worth, when it seems that only the runt of the single litter shows any interest in you. But I want to encourage you to activate your 'treasure factor'. The above scripture is so fitting, because I believe that no matter what your little heart has been made to endure, it is not unfit for service. It is not damaged goods. The mere fact that you decided to pick up this book, or still desire marriage shows that, although you were afflicted in every way, you were not crushed; although you were left perplexed, you were not driven to despair; although you were persecuted, you were not forsaken; and although this world's love has struck you down, you were not destroyed.

I remember a few times in my life when I had to tell myself that I would love again. Lara Fabian's song became my anthem on more than one occasion. This song and its lyrics picked me up a few times. I would sing it as I drove, with tears streaming down my face. I would belt it out and as the tempo rose, so would my hope. I believed with all my heart that I would love again. I knew that on the other side of whatever had broken my heart, I was still worthy of the relationship that I pursued, and that I was one step closer to my forever. I did however change one of the lines in the song to suit my heart.

"I will love again

Though my heart is breaking, I will love again

Stronger than before

I will love again

Even if it takes a lifetime to get over you.

No! it won't take a lifetime to get over you [my line]

Heaven only knows, I will love again."

I sang it after my love of six years died of cancer. I sang it after my divorce was final. I sang it after my son's father rejected us. I believed, so I spoke. One thing that has kept me, in many of these instances was my speech – IS my speech. Always remember that you cannot have what you speak against. This is a rule I have lived by. You need to start speaking *those things that be not, as though they were* (Romans 4), and you need stop blocking yourself. You block yourself by saying things that are contrary to what you desire.

I remember once posting a meme I found funny, because it was absolutely true for my life "Beyoncé has been 'crazy in love', 'dangerously in love' and 'drunk in love' and I can't even find a guy I like." It seemed innocent and just funny, but I had such inner turmoil while it was posted. Only after I had removed it did I find a bit of peace. I didn't realize it at the time, but it was the Holy Spirit letting me know that we were not in agreement over this subject that I had handed over to Him.

I also realized that I didn't want to be crazy in love, or drunk in love or dangerously in love. For some reason we have romanticized volatility and instability. No, I want to be sanely in love, soberly in love and securely in love. I don't want all that teen angst about 'he loves me, he loves me not'. I want the sobriety of experiencing and enjoying every single moment of a good healthy love that leads me toward healthy and whole decisions, not drunken regrets. I don't want that asylum-type love that binds me to hugging myself and to incoherent chatter that is devoid of truth. I don't want that kind of love that numbs the senses and keeps me in a catatonic state.

It took me a while to get back into the habit of aligning my actions and words to my desires after my last disappointment and rejection. But I did get back on it.

I remember a call from my baby sister in which she was relaying her desires for her baby shower. She stated that she wanted something small and intimate and that there would be a separate 'Pampers party' for the males in our family. I immediately told her that I didn't know if my husband would be attending, but would let her know closer to the time. She responded by saying that he would definitely be there, as he loved spending time with his brothers-in-law. Although this was just playful banter, I felt a spark in my spirit. The Holy Spirit was nudging my speech. I had given the 'husband search' over to Him, and He had responded in straightening out my talk. I realized how blessed I was to have my family 'faith along' with me. To others it would seem as though they were just playing along but my happiness and my forever after is not a game to them. It was a matter of faith, so they 'faith alongside me'. They speak of my husband in the now. They include his presence in our plans. That's the power of agreement. Not only that, it fills me with excitement, and continually renews my hope.

Young's Literal Translation of 2 Corinthians 4:7 states, *And we have this treasure in earthen vessels, that the excellency of the power may be of God, and not of us;*

The EXCELLENCY of the TREASURE that is in you, is of God, and not of you, so there is nothing that you can do, or that has been done to you, that can diminish its continued worth. Your heart might have been broken, but take heart in this, it was broken wide open for the love of God to shine in and to show you what love really is, and what it should be. You need to heal, and allow God to put you back together again.

Once, as I was looking for things to help me heal, I came across this post: "You don't know this new me; I put back my pieces, differently." (@highpoetsociety) This one spoke to me on a spiritual level, and I want it to speak to you too. This quote is directed to the person who hurt you, but let me put this to you: Are you not tired of attracting the same kind of man? The law of attraction states that 'like attracts like'. This means that people with a low frequency – people who are insecure and self-abandoning – attract each other, while people with a high frequency – people who love and value themselves also attract each other. #Boom! Mindblown!

Psalm Isadora in her article *Why You Keep Attracting the Wrong Partners* explains that "We attract what we think we deserve. And what we think we deserve is usually rooted in what we experienced or witnessed in our early childhood development."

She goes on further to give ways to break the cycle, which include:

1. Recognizing your patterns.
2. Stop re-enacting the past.
3. Own it.
4. Believe you deserve it.
5. Open your heart.

All of which I agree with, but going back to my quote, I'd like to draw your attention to another kind of Psalm:

Psalm 147 NLT

1. 1 Praise the LORD! How good to sing praises to our God! How delightful and how fitting!
2. The LORD is rebuilding Jerusalem and bringing the exiles back to Israel.
3. He heals the brokenhearted and bandages their wounds.
4. He counts the stars and calls them all by name. Of verses 3-4 Young's Literal Translation (YLT) says:
5. Who is giving healing to the broken of heart, And is binding up their grief's.
6. Appointing the number of the stars, To all them He giveth names.

Here God is rebuilding Jerusalem. Other words for rebuilding are transforming, upgrading, renewing, rejuvenating, and causing a revolution. You, in this instance, are Jerusalem. Not only is He putting back your pieces differently, God is also busy setting you up for revolution, for a renewal of heart and mind and soul. He is rejuvenating you so that your heart is made young again, and loves like it's never been hurt, the way it is supposed to be. God is also *bringing the exiles back*. Those things and feelings and hopes that were exiled in the hurt, God is restoring. Those principles, such as purity, and waiting, that were exiled as being old fashioned are being restored. God is giving healing, but it's your responsibility to receive it. He is binding and bandaging up your griefs and wounds. He is setting the broken things in a cast, so that they are not touched while healing happens.

But look at verse 4 which seems so out of place here: *He counts the stars and calls them all by name*. I believe this seemingly random verse is there because when healing is complete, you become the star the brilliant, celebrated, shining treasure of heaven that you are. And He calls you by name; by a new name. God is not foolish. He will not restore you and renew you, only to send you back out there to those who don't understand your worth. No, He puts you where like attracts like.

I once read a quote that went something along the lines of, "You can't expect to be treated like a Louboutin, when you act like a flip flop". It's funny, but it's true. Or it's funny and it's true. Or it's funny because it's true. See what I did there? Live in your new worth. Stop being a flip flop when God has done all He can to make you into a Louboutin.

No-one has to tell you that a diamond is valuable. The diamond doesn't go around trying to convince anyone of its worth. The diamond isn't putting up a red flag, to make it easier for miners to find them. No, they do none of that. They are simply diamonds. They may be buried deep in the dirt, where no-one can see their shine, but you know what? That has never stopped a prospector from wanting it, from seeking after it, from giving up everything to have it. That's the 'Find'.

You are not 'found' as wife because you were in plain sight; you are not found as a wife because you successfully convinced someone of your worth. No, you are found because you are valuable. You are found because you are sought after, pursued, hunted. You are found because someone is actively looking for all that you are and have. The worth of the treasure pulls the heart of the hunter, and he won't give up, until he has found her.

When you discover and live in your worth, you attract the merchant, who knows treasure. He is looking and seeking and searching anyway. It's in him, it's his hunger. And suddenly, those trinket seeking scavengers fade away. They will not dare stand in the way of the man who knows what he wants.

Know who you are.

Your husband is the merchant. You are the diamond.

Your husband is the hunter. You are the sought after item.

Your husband is the pursuer. You are the responder.

What does the Bible say about man as the pursuer?

When I looked for synonyms of the phrase 'sought after', I came across the most beautifully fitting and descriptive words: adored, preferred, chosen, desired, singled out, hunted, required.

As I pointed out earlier in this book, Adam was already pursuing Eve long before he met her. I believe he was searching for her. He already knew that he required her. I believe the desire in him was already awoken when he saw how everything in nature had its counterpart. He could have chosen anyone of these that he had dominion over, but he preferred to wait for Eve. And when he saw her, he adored her, and his adoration claimed her. When your Adam sees you, your gift and individual treasure will single you out from them all.

Even when God brought Eve to Adam, he still had to look into her, take ownership of her, by giving her a name that was tied to his name, and he had to draw the wife out of her by his recognition of himself in her.

This truth of pursuit and adoration is not confined to Genesis. The entire book of Song of Solomon is a striking, graphic picture of a bridegroom pursuing his love. He initiates their relationship and she responds to his tender courtship. It's a beautiful dance of catch and release.

Another story that reveals this truth, is that of Hosea and Gomer – the story of the prophet of God who married a prostitute. He went out and found her, rescued her from a life of sin and shame and married her. Again and again Gomer returns to her past life, and again and again Hosea pursues her. The first time he went after her, he left behind everything to have her. Again and again he goes back and even pays a hefty price to purchase her back. He continually pursues, she responds, although her response is not always positive.

But why? Why did God created men as pursuers and woman as responders?

God's design of masculinity as pursuer of femininity directly reflects Christ's pursuit of his bride, the church. Jesus pursued us, his bride (1 John 4:19). Male and female directly reflect Christ's pursuit of his bride. *Husbands, love your wives, as Christ loved the church and gave himself up for her, that he might sanctify her, having cleansed her by the washing of water with the word, so that he might present the church to himself in splendour, without spot or wrinkle or any such thing, that she might be holy and without blemish.* (Eph. 5:25-32)

The entire Bible, from Genesis to Revelation is a love story of how God has pursued and wooed his people and the church. The Church and Christ, and the Husband and wife.

I believe that God's primary reason for creating man was not for man to worship Him. Now I know that sounds like a blasphemous statement, but the opposite sounds like a vain, insecure god to me. Before you close this book and call me a heretic, hear out my reasoning and decide for yourself.

We are definitely called to worship God, but to my understanding, man was created primarily to commune with God.

God already had thousands upon thousands of angles worshiping before Him day and night; revering Him, calling out "Holy Holy Holy, to Him who was, who is and who is to come". He had Lucifer, whom many scholars believe to be the first and most anointed worship leader before the Fall. But none of them walked the Garden with Him and talked with Him as Adam did. None of them had access to God the Father the way Adam did. Adam was the first of his kind. There was nothing in the entire universe more like God than Adam, so why would God need to make a replica of Himself to worship Him? He didn't. God created Adam for a purpose different from what the angels were already doing. He was created as a companion.

Our first and primary reason for creation is laid out clear as day in the Great Commandment. *And He [Jesus] replied to him: you shall love the Lord your God with all your heart and with all your soul and with all your mind [intellect].* (Matthew 22:37) So important is this that in Deuteronomy 6 from verse 4 where it is first mentioned, Moses tells Israel that it ought to be the first thought in their own hearts and minds, and then they are to impress it on their children as engraved in them. They are instructed to talk about them when they sit at home or walk in the street, when they lay down and when they got up. They were to tie them as symbols on their hands and foreheads; they were to write it on the door frames of their houses and gates. Everywhere they looked and went they needed to see this commandment. This love was to be all consuming. But isn't that what love is? When we fall in love, isn't that what it's like? God created us to love Him, and to do so willingly. Yes, worship would flow from that love automatically, but God wanted Communion with man. He already had access to 24/7 worship.

I know it's not as simple as I am about to state it, nor do I have the biblical theory and reference points to support it but I firmly believe that when God saw Adam and Eve together in the Garden, He saw the communion He had longed for in His creation of Adam. I believe He saw the oneness and intimacy and His longing for it only grew. And it was for this reason that He decided upon the Church. God decided upon a bride for Himself.

God is for marriage. He advocates for it, and He fights for it, and He protects it. He has gone into the schoolyard like a big brother to defend it and to warn those who would try to dismantle it. *What God has put together, let not man separate.* (Matthew 19:6) That is a warning whose consequences have not been explicitly divulged. The kind of warning that says 'you don't want to know what I will do to those who do this.' Hebrews 13:4 tells us *Let marriage be held in honour [esteemed worthy, precious, of great price and especially dear] in all things...* Marriage is the only thing that God looked at and decided to create one for Himself. God honoured marriage so much that He wanted it for himself.

And that's what this whole thing is. From beginning to end, it's Gods pursuit of us. He knows our value, and all He wants is to have us. All He wants is for us to willingly be His.

Chapter 10
OBTAINS FAVOUR

I guess the first question I would ask myself is: What is the benefit of favour? If a man who finds a wife obtains favour, I would want to know what this favour is, and what it does for me. It seems the answer would be an obvious one, but the lack of committing men in this day and age would suggest otherwise. If this one act, which is so unassuming, would provide men with the favour of God, don't you think men everywhere would be falling over themselves to get married, in order to assure themselves the obtainment of this favour? I think the lack of understanding of this statement, and the promise attached to it is what has kept men from their glory.

We all know that the 5th commandment states to *honour your mother and father, so that you may live long in the land the LORD your God is giving you.* We famously quote this as the only commandment with a promise attached, and we would be right, but I think we ought to approach Proverbs 18:22 in the same way. If we do A, we are promised B. Both of these apply to horizontal relationships with a vertical promise. If you correctly approach these particular human-to- human relationships, you are promised a heavenly reward. In the case of Proverbs 18:22 that reward means favour.

This is how biblestudytools.com describes 'favour' "Finding favour means gaining approval, acceptance, or special benefits or blessings... The favour that human beings receive from God depends on his good pleasure..."

Let's take a look at what the favour of God afforded some of the men in the Bible.

There are those to whom God showed exceptional favour, and looking at sacred text we can learn more about what it is that attracts the heart and favour of God. What makes certain people favourites?

Let's start with Enoch.

All the Bible says about Enoch was that *he walked with God, and was no more, for God took him.* (Genesis 5: 21-24)

Quantity, quality, and proximity. These were the three words that popped up in my spirit with respect to this scripture.

Because I believe that God primarily created us for companionship with Him, it makes absolute sense to me that when we lavish our attention on God, we activate favour. Enoch walked with God. I believe the amount of time he spent with God surpassed the amount of time he spent with anything and anyone else. Quantity.

I also believe that the time he spent with God was special to God. Yes, it was special to Enoch, but Tommy Tenney, in his book *The God Chasers* states that "While we seek God encounters, God seeks man encounters." I believe this is what Enoch gave God. He gave God quality encounters. He gave God the best of himself and of his time. He wasn't ticking off 'spend time with God' as another chore he had to finish. His heart was completely in it. He was enamoured by God, and it showed. Quality.

Because of this time spent walking with God, I'm sure they talked and talked, and laughed, and shared many things. The more God spoke, the closer Enoch came to understanding the heart of God.

The more Enoch understood, the more God shared. Do you know how good it feels to 'click' with someone? To be able to connect on that level? Well it feels good for God too, and I believe it's because of this that God swooped down and grabbed Enoch to be with Him. The intimacy created in those moments caused God to shorten the time in waiting to be together. God wanted closer proximity. And He wanted it now.

Gods favour was evident in Enoch's life – mainly by his early rapture – and was activated by quantity, quality, and proximity.

For Noah, the favour of God on his life caused him, and his offspring (his lineage, future generations) to be spared from the judgement of the flood.

"Noah was a righteous man, blameless among the people of his time, and he walked with God." (Genesis 6: 9)

Noah, in my book, should also have been credited with being a 'father of faith', because he just as easily obeyed the voice of God, to do as God commanded, without knowing; and it was from Noah's seed that came the people who are *scattered over the earth* (Genesis 9:19). Added to that, dominion was once again given into his hands, and he was given the blessing of increase. (Genesis 9: 1-3, 7) But Noah's obedience was used to purge, while Abraham's obedience was used to replenish. Noah was righteous, and

Abraham's faith in God was credited to him as righteousness. It's an archetypal progression of relationship.

For Abraham, the favour of God on his life cannot even be properly calculated. Let's look at the aspects of favour shown to Abraham in Genesis 12:2-3 –

- *I will make you into a great nation (a legacy greater than even he could imagine)*

- *And I will bless you (continued influx of God's blessing)*

- *I will make your name great, (your good reputation will precede you)*

- *And you will be a blessing (an outpouring of the excess of the influx of the blessing of God. Because Abraham was himself a blessing, everything he touched prospered, every dry well he dug produced water.)*

- *I will bless those who bless you (a Godly partnership with those who have your best interest at heart– mutually beneficial relationships and partnerships. A magnet for good connections)*

- *And whoever curses you I will curse (God will fight your cause/case for you)*

- *And all the peoples of the earth will be blessed through you (speaks to legacy and heritage, but more than that speaks to your place as a legal vessel / pathway for God to release heaven on earth.)*

If that isn't mind blowing enough, when we fast forward to chapter 15 of Genesis we see another promise as a result of favour.

Do not be afraid Abram, I am your shield, (continually, never moving, never allowing an unprotected moment) *[I am] Your very great reward* (God gives Himself to Abram, along with all His powers, resources – both natural and spiritual – and His abilities. (Genesis 15:1)

We sing William McDowells' *I give myself away* at the top of our lungs, not thinking that there is a mutuality to that statement, that God too wants to take advantage of. God wants to give Himself to us in an all-consuming manner, as a reward, because we are all-consumed by and with Him.

All of this is very lofty, but this same favour made room for Abraham to ask for the one thing he desperately wanted – an heir from his own loins. (Genesis 15: 3-4) Rather than pay attention to the request made by Abram, consider the access, boldness and confidence Abraham was afforded to be able to ask God for a solid demand. Favour gave Abraham access to the throne room, so that, in accordance with 1 John 5:14, he had the confidence to approach God, knowing that whatever he asked in God's will, God would not only hear, but God would grant.

Wouldn't that be something incredible to have? For many of us, just the guarantee that God hears us, is enough to reduce us to tears of relief, affirmation and joy. Now add to that the confidence, the unwavering certainty of knowing that what you have asked is already yours.

What we also know is that Abram not only knew who God was, but also that he had a solid relationship with Him. We know this because chapter 12 and verse 1 of Genesis states that *The Lord said to Abram*... This denotes that there had been at least one prior conversation, and that Abram was not shocked with the voice from the sky. Abram's immediate obedience, without question to the given instruction, also supports my theory that Abram was acquainted with God. Abram had known the God of his forefathers.

I am sure the story of Noah was one that had been told and retold generation after generation. I am sure the habit of worship of this God was carried down to every new member of the bloodline. Abram believed because of the word of the testimony. Long before he became the father of many nations, and way before the promise, he already proved to be someone who believed in this God in the absence of proof, just going on a hand-me-down-faith. That's all he needed. So when God told him to leave, he didn't question it. It may be concluded that because of this blind obedience and trust, that God gave Abram his own personal encounter with Him.

The LORD appeared to Abram... (v 7) By way of contrast, there is no record of the Lord appearing to Noah.

In my mind's eye, I see Abram as this person who has a pen pal far away; someone he knows is powerful and royal. He receives advice from this person, and comfort and guidance. One day this faraway friend tells him to go to the airport and wait there. Abram's trust in their established relationship spurs him on to follow the instruction, not knowing what he will find there. But once there, Abram gets to meet this friend in person. Finally. I know it's a very one dimensional metaphor, but that is what I see when I read this passage. The basis

of it from God's vantage point is Abram's trust in God. The basis of it from Abram's vantage point is God's revelation of Himself to the newly named Abraham. That one on one encounter caused him to see himself as God sees him, unleashing in him an energy that went from potential to kinetic – a force to be reckoned with. But not only that, he suddenly had the weight of heaven as his backing, because God Himself counted him among His friends. (James 2:23)

Remember my earlier quote? *He who finds a WIFE, finds a good thing* – not he who finds a girl looking for a ring.

I want to take you back to the treasure seeker – the man looking for treasure. That man is our David. The God seeker, the man after God's heart. Enoch happened upon a relationship with God. Noah's right living and obedience to the law, got God's attention. Abraham's blind trust made him a friend of God. With Joseph, the favour of God on his life, gave him prominence and promotion wherever he found himself, whether in Potiphar's house, or the prison, and even the palace. It's one thing being a big fish in a small pond; that's easy. But it's a totally different thing being set up to dominate in every arena regardless of its size.

Yet David… promiscuous, adulterating, impulsive, murderous, faltering David… Yes he trusted, and yes he obeyed, but following the law was something that seemed a bit optional to him. David was a treasure seeker, and he was a treasure attracter. He danced with God. He drew God in with worship, and praise, then he chased after God with heart and soul. That is the kind of treasure seeker you deserve. If a man recognizes a relationship with God as the ultimate treasure, he will have no problem recognizing the treasure in you. And that man knows that because you are valuable, you add value. What is valuable can only enhance and add value. Gold prospectors of old knew this one thing: "If I could possess one gold nugget, I can own fields, and livestock, I can expand my territory, and with that expand my influence. I can employ workers, and I can enhance the lives of others." That's what that one gold nugget could do.

There is a famous quote by American author Erick S. Gray that, at one point had been circling on social media. It states: "Whatever you give a woman, she will make greater. If you give her sperm, she'll give you a baby. If you give her a house, she'll give you a home. If you give her groceries, she'll give you a meal. If you give her a smile, she'll give you her heart. She multiplies and enlarges what is given to her..." I believe this statement to carry immense truth. Just like that one gold nugget represents everything that can be realized with attaining it – or finding it – so I believe woman, and more importantly wife, possesses within her everything that is needed to obtain those things for which man seeks and desires.

That's one facet of the favour a wife can bring to the table.

The other side of this coin is *of the Lord/ from the Lord*. There is favour, and then there is God's favour. God's favour is the kind of favour that is termed unfair or unbalanced to the human understanding. Deuteronomy 6:10-11 gives us an example of that kind of favour.

When the LORD your God brings you into the land he swore to your fathers, to Abraham, Isaac and Jacob, to give you – a land with large, flourishing cities you did not build, 11 houses filled with all kinds of good things you did not provide, wells you did not dig, and vineyards and olive groves you did not plant – then when you eat and are satisfied...

The law of sowing and reaping determines that *whatsoever a man soweth that he shall also reap* (Galatians 6:7), in fact the Bible is very clear that *As long as the earth endures, seedtime and harvest, cold and heat, summer and winter, day and night will never cease* (Genesis 8:22). In other words, there are the things that happen as a result of the amount of work we have put in, or for the level of obedience we adhere to, as is the case in Joshua 1:8. This is a certain kind of favour. I would call this 'normal favour'. Normal in that it is stipulated according to the Word of God that this is how a child of God should be living and operating in, on a daily basis. Normal because to a certain degree it is activated by us, our actions (obedience) and the law of returns. Now this could sound like one doesn't need God because a man's hard work could get him everything he desired. But do not forget, that it is God who causes the sun to shine on the seed, and causes favourable conditions for the seed to grow, and ultimately gives the life inside that seed in order for it to produce. That's His favour coupled with your work.

Then there is a deeper level of favour. The kind you get when you are a David or an Abraham, or an Enoch. This has nothing to do with what you do. It is not an exorbitant reward for labour but has everything to do with who you are associated with. These are the lands with large, flourishing cities you did not build, and the houses filled with all kinds of good things you did not provide or the wells you did not dig, and vineyards and olive groves you did not plant, that will be yours, that are yours and have been pre-prepared in advance for you. Can a wife do this, you ask? Absolutely. Why? Because God honours the wife. Let's look at 1 Peter 3:7 –

Likewise, ye husbands, dwell withthem according toknowledge, giving honour unto the wife, as unto the weaker vessel, and as being heirs together of the grace of life; that your prayers be not hindered. (KJV)

The same goes for you husbands: Be good husbands to your wives. Honour them, delight in them. As women they lack some of your advantages. But in the new life of God's grace, you're equals. Treat your wives, then, as equals so your prayers don't run aground. (The Message MSG)

What I want to draw your attention to firstly, is the consequence of not living in understanding with, or honouring the wife: the prayers of husband are hindered or run aground. Imagine that. Imagine not even being able to call on God to get you out. Imagine God blocking his ears to your cry, to your plea? Isn't that favouritism when God chooses not to hear the prayer of one person based on his actions toward another person? In no other relationship is this prevalent. Children are disobedient all the time, workers dishonour their superiors all the time, but God does not warn them that their prayers will be hindered. Why is that? Because as I said earlier, in marriage, God sees both of you or He sees neither of you.

I don't want to dwell too much on the role of the husband, but I do want you to understand how much God honours you as wife, so much so that He would dare to disturb His relationship and communication with husband until he too takes on the position of honouring you.

Wayne Grudem in his commentary on 1 Peter has made this insightful remark: "So concerned is God that Christian husbands live in an understanding and loving way with their wives, that he 'interrupts' his relationship with them when they are not doing so. No Christian husband should presume to think that any spiritual good will be accomplished by his life without an effective ministry of prayer. And no husband may expect an effective prayer life unless he lives with his wife 'in an understanding way, bestowing honour' on her. To take the time to develop and maintain a good marriage is God's will; it is serving God; it is a spiritual activity pleasing in his sight." (Wayne Grudem, 1 Peter, p. 146.)

Can you think of anything more vital and important than your unbroken communion with God? When a husband's relationship with wife is not right, this breaks his communion with God.

How and why are you honoured?

Firstly, you are to be honoured as the weaker vessel.

A vessel is a jug or a container or a bowl; any sort of receptacle that houses something. So in other words, you are to be treated outwardly as fragile, with gentleness, and tenderness and care, to be protected and valued, and placed in a position of safety. What you house is not weak, not by any stretch of imagination, but the vessel is.

Secondly, being an heir; being a literal princess.

Meghan Markle has nothing on you, child. You are the daughter of the King of the entire universe, and you are about to inherit everything He has for you, and you should thus be treated as the royal you are. You are a person of worth and value to God, because you are

His daughter. God expects your husband to show you honour by lifting you up in his esteem and acknowledging your value in the sight of God and all around him. Failure to do so causes a block in communication between him and God.

Wife is a gateway to God, just like wife is a gateway to Husband. You hurt her, you hurt Gods heart. You honour her, you receive honour, and you receive favour that is above and beyond all that you could think or imagine. God honours Wife; He placed great value in her. That value adds value to everything she touches. It adds value to the life of Husband.

I never really agreed with the phrase, 'happy wife, happy life' because it's a spoilt child mentality, but in the context of this verse, it could apply, but I would say it's more to the point, to say 'honoured wife, honoured life'.

When God applies His honour to the life of Husband because of Wife, you can unequivocally call that favour. The getting of wells you did not dig... things that have been in the line of the King of Kings, and handed down to generations of kings, who became so by finding their queen, and giving her a name of greater honour – wife.

You are the favour. You are the manifestation of God's presence in the life of your husband.

Chapter 11
GOD SAVE THE KING

When the king has abdicated.

I just want to divert here for a second, and address the single women like myself, who are raising boys, raising kings, and are at the same time opening their hearts to love again.

This child that I have, Zadoq-Levi Alexander Scoble, is a complete and whole blessing from God. He is a king. Yes, he was born out of wedlock, but he is a king nonetheless, because at the end of it all, only God can give life. But... but it is not Gods will for us, firstly, to have kids outside of the confines and covering of a marriage and the two parent structure He has set in place, and secondly, it's not in His will or in the best interest of these children that they be raised in a broken family held together by visitation sessions and custody agreements. Having Zadoq-Levi has made me a parent. Having him outside of Holy parameters has labelled me a single parent.

I read a post on someone's WhatsApp status once that just grabbed me at the throat and demanded my attention. It was a screenshot and was devoid of any source information. Here is that post

"People should stop calling themselves 'single mothers'. Have you ever seen a 'double mother' or a triple mother'? No. You are a MOTHER. Motherhood is complete and perfect. Motherhood does not presuppose marital bliss. You are a mother. You may be a single woman (suggesting that you are looking for a partner). You may be celibate. These states have nothing to do with your motherhood. Your children have a complete mother as any other children. A father is not an associate mother. A man does not take away or increase that perfect vocation of motherhood. Adjust your attitude and speech accordingly."

Upon reading the first line of this post, I immediately wanted to jump on my high horse and respond to the poster. It may not have been their words, but it was their sentiment, and I felt that no-one had any right to say anything to or about 'single moms'. But as I continued to read, I felt the Holy Spirit nudge me, first rebuking me, and then affirming something He had told me long ago. The rebuke was that in God's original plan for me, and for every mother, motherhood *does* presuppose marital bliss. This is God's order of events.

When I first found out that I was pregnant and then found that I would be doing this alone, I resolved within myself that I would not be both mom and dad to my son. I knew that if I tried to do that my son would lose both mother and father while I failed dismally at trying to juggle both roles. I knew that stepping out of my role, even halfway, would rob my son of a whole mother, and it would rob me of the essence of being a woman in my entirety, so I made a covenant with God: I'll be the best mother I can be to this boy You have given me, and You Lord, will take care of the Father part...

A few hours later when I was reading the Word of God in my daily devotional, with a broken and despondent heart, God spoke to me in this... Psalm 2:7-8 He said to me *You are my son, today I have become your Father. Ask of Me, and I will make the nations your inheritance and the ends of the earth your possession*. I knew immediately that God was speaking to the little person in my tummy, and when my son was born, and I was in my feelings hoping baby's daddy would come back, God reminded me of His promise once again, and He keeps on reminding me whenever I forget.

But being human, and even with this promise, I still felt that my son was missing an 'audible' voice in his life. I knew GOD would do as He had promised, but in the now, in this moment, I felt that there was no voice to speak to my tummy, and no earthly father to welcome him. I wanted him to have a voice that he could recognise as he came into this world – a man's voice. To be truthful, it wasn't really my son who was missing out on an audible voice, it was just me being overwhelmed by a wave of emotions as I had always imagined my husband speaking to my belly during pregnancy. Not having that caused me to opt for other means of audible voices. So I would play sermons from TD Jakes' *He Motions* conference to my belly, and later when my son was born, I would play his *ManPower* series as my son slept. I tried my best, and continue to do so, to make sure that my little king has plenty of time with male role models, and I find those in my own father and my brothers-in-law, as well as in key male members of my extended family.

It then dawned on me that my new reality introduced me to a world that I had heard about, seen around me, but never really knew anything about. I had read the statistics, and had seen the effect of fatherless homes in many African American movies, but it was not something I believed I would ever need to worry about. I grew up with both my parents and the alternative was never an option. But here I was with a son, and no king in the home.

While single parenthood is not easy for anyone, mothers of boys have an additional burden: they are often especially stigmatized. Researchers have found that when kids grow up in single-parent homes, boys are affected more adversely than girls, especially when the available parent is the mother. According to the report, *Wayward Sons: The Emerging Gender Gap in Labor Markets and Education*, published on the *Third Way Organization* website, the sons of single parents may experience financial, emotional, social and psychological issues. "After all, doesn't prevailing wisdom claim that boys who grow up without fathers turn out to be helpless sissies, violent adults, or gay?"(Peggy Drexler, author of *Raising Boys Without Men: How Maverick Moms Are Creating the Next Generation of Exceptional Men*, and research psychologist and assistant professor of psychology at the US Cornell University's Weill Medical College.)

In everything I read with regard to my role as a single female parent raising a son, I shuddered at what the world was saying about my little future king. Yet, once again, I was reminded of my Promise, my covenant with God, and was comforted that my covenant ensured me that my son would not be a statistic. No matter how long I needed to wait for my husband and kinsman redeemer to find us, my son would be safe. The voice in his head is God.

My son is blessed enough to be a Moses in the reeds, but there still needs to be a king in the home. It is for this reason that my relationship with the King of kings has to be extremely exposed. My prayers have to be audible, my conversations with my God have to be visible; God's hand and voice in my life has to be evidently noticeable; my life has to be a testimony in my home, because my son needs to see the King in the house. There are very few quiet closeted prayers. Each need, each concern, each thankful heart has to be raised up in a voice and conversation that my son recognizes as speaking to the Almighty, and although he is so young, each victory is explained to him, as though he knew what we were believing God for. I have to make the king in my home visible to my son, because we produce after our own kind. Our children become what they see. I do not want a little almost-male version of myself walking around in my son. He was never made to be a queen.

But how can he see what a king is, when the king has abdicated?

Killing the King.

There are many women just like me, who, for whatever reason are raising boys in the absence of a father. There is no king in the home, and unfortunately the prevalent means of dealing with it, is either placing him under a 'pharaoh', or going it alone.

Pharaoh is that man who enters the relationship with a woman who has a child/ren. Instead of loving those children and nurturing them, and honouring their life and assisting in their purpose, he sees them as a threat or as a rival, and does everything he can to 'kill' them. They demoralize, and abuse, and exclude and diminish. You don't have to be a genius to know that the children are not his.

My family has been and is still very anxious to see me married. Not because they feel sorry for me, or want to get rid of me, but because they want to see me happy. My desire for marriage and family is something that has been evident in me for yonks, but more than that, their desperation for me is spurred on because I have a son, and he needs a king in the house.

I share this sentiment: It was not part of the plan to be alone. I am made for marriage and family, and God knows, I dream of the man who is going to teach my son to be a king – who is going to teach him how to harness the power within himself to rule over what God has laid ahead of him. But that is a mammoth task.

I cannot kill the king because I am lonely and don't want to be alone. I need to consider the king. I need to consider the king on either side of me. The king my son is to be, and the king who is to be my husband. (In the natural and Godly order of events, one would consider the king in your husband, and the king your son is to be.) But in my desire for a kinsman redeemer, I cannot kill the king by settling for a pharaoh. I have seen too many women settle for a man, any man, to soothe the sting of loneliness and provide that feeling of acceptance, belonging and completeness, at a very high price.

I once dated a guy, whose own father had absconded, and his mother was in a relationship with a man who was the very definition of pharaoh. My then beau was a beautiful young man who was extremely lost and dejected. He didn't want to be anything like the man who had abandoned his mother and himself, and had no connection with the man sharing his mother's bed. It was a constant battle for her love and attention, and finding his role in this new makeshift family. There was a tornado inside of him, always whirling. Because he had come to salvation in Jesus Christ, he was learning what a father and a king should be. It was difficult for him to reconcile what he saw around him with what the Word of God and the voice of God was saying to him. What he knew for sure was that this man who had embedded himself into his mother's life had no intention of showing him, or his sister, any fatherly love. These kids that this woman had were just a nuisance that he could have done without. Unfortunately and very sadly, his mother had deep hurts of her own, and could not identify the damage that this pharaoh was inflicting upon her and her kids. All she wanted was to be loved, and accepted. If only she knew what love was, then she'd know that this wasn't it.

I have often thought of this relationship, especially since raising my own son. I saw what that pharaoh was doing to the king inside this kid. Even at such a young and immature age myself, I could see the effect on this young man – the bewilderment in his eyes and in his decision making. He was already operating on fewer cylinders with the rejection and desertion by his biological father, and then was further dejected, spurned, and crushed by the man who irresponsibly held his mother's heart, caused him to vacillate between being her protector, falling short under the weight of that task, and just hoping to find his place as her beloved son. This young would-be king was under subjection to a pharaoh.

I have prayed many intense prayers, guarding my heart against loneliness that would give a pharaoh the slightest gap, to try and oppress me and kill my little king.

Ladies, please, God has a king for you; don't settle for a pharaoh.

Especially if you are raising little kings. Don't marry the wrong guy. As a single parent, REALLY don't marry the wrong guy. It's one thing to make decisions that derail your path and purpose, but a completely different atrocity to make a decision that derails the path and purpose of your children, and even worse when they are hurt and scarred mentally, physically, emotionally or spiritually, because of a decision that they have had no control over.

Now, this scenario is not true of all men who take on the role of what we call 'step-father' but it is true of the pharaoh that slides into this role.

Just to side step for a second, I am often asked if I would encourage my son to call my husband 'daddy', knowing that his paternal parent is still alive and out there somewhere. My response and my thinking is: "Yes, absolutely!" Dad, or father, is not the biological contribution; it's a role and designation, and my kinsman redeemer is the man who not only loves me, but loves my son, not 'as his own', which is merely a predetermined disclaimer that he is not his own. It's the man who loves my son like I love my son, like God loves my son, as he loves himself. Period. It is for this reason that I have always imagined telling my son to "give this to your father" or "go tell your father..." not your step-father. There will no dashes in my family. None. If I am to be his wife, and he is to be my husband, then this is to be our son, and this unit, our Family. There will be no dashes in my family. No separations at all.

Another of God's promises to me. Personally.

My disclaimer: I have no idea of the dynamic that has left any other woman a single parent, or what God has determined their parental plan to be according to their circumstances. This is just my promise.

But back to pharaoh.

The thing with pharaoh is that he is not God appointed. His biggest role is to oppress the children of God, to make slaves out of them and to kill the king. The killing of the king is not a new concept.

In fact, if you could see the translucent strand that has been threaded down through the ages to dismantle the family and

170

dethrone the king, you would be shocked at how obvious it has been.

Saving the king

Then Pharaoh, the king of Egypt, gave this order to the Hebrew midwives, Shiphrah and Puah: "When you help the Hebrew women as they give birth, watch as they deliver. If the baby is a boy, kill him; if it is a girl, let her live." (Exodus 1:15-16 NLT)

In our text, Pharaoh knew that a deliverer would rise up among the ones he had oppressed and afflicted, and he wanted to make sure that that did not happen. In my limited understanding, reading this in depth for the first time as a teen, trying my own Bible study, I wondered why Pharaoh didn't just kill the women. After all, it's the women who bear the children, and if you prevented them from bearing children, you could circumvent the birth of a redeemer. By killing the male children, he was just weakening his own future work force. That was my thinking until I came to understand the difference between a seed carrier and an incubator.

Everything needed for vast vineyards is found within a single seed. If you stop the seed, you stop the vineyard. The seed houses the vineyard. The seed houses the oak. This story of annihilation is also a plot for defiling the bloodline, for changing the trajectory of the story of salvation and redemption.

Pharaoh knew that he needed to eliminate this entire nation, but to add insult to injury he wanted to strengthen his own nation, by eventually using the Israelite woman as incubators of the Egyptian seed; A new generation of the pharaonic bloodline, or a tailor-made workforce, using Gods chosen people just as a final slap in the face.

Killing of the male child did not end when Pharoah didn't get his way, in fact it was the same tactic Herod employed when he heard of Jesus' birth.

When Herod realized that he had been outwitted by the Magi, he was furious, and he gave orders to kill all the boys in Bethlehem and its vicinity who were two years old and under, in accordance with the time he had learned from the Magi. Then what was said through the prophet Jeremiah was fulfilled: "A voice is heard in Ramah, weeping and great mourning, Rachel weeping for her children and refusing to be comforted, because they are no more." (Matthew 2:16-18 NIV)

This 'killing of the king' is still very much prevalent today. Just because Jesus came, doesn't mean that Satan gave up. He's not going to give up until the end of time. He killed the king once, or at least he thought he did, when Jesus willingly gave his life. But that resulted in resurrection and a whole new breed of Christians who now have the keys to the kingdom of heaven, who now have all authority to loose and to bind. (Matthew 16:19) But Satan's aim is still to kill the king.

What happens when the king is killed?

During times when kings and fighting men made their way to gruesome battlefields, having a ruler fall in combat was by no means unheard of. In fact, prior to the age of muskets, kings and princes would often lead their armies from the front, exposing themselves to many of the same risks faced by their men. In any case, with the king slain, the defeated army fled the field and eventually ceded control of their armed forces and their land and territory to the opposing foe, who would then also seize the throne. With seizing the throne, everything that was under rule of that king was now subject to the new conqueror. The people ruled by the fallen king were now made to be slaves or completely eradicated. In Bible times, they were often forced to worship false gods, exiled to foreign lands, and were subject to a life of servitude. Battles were fought and re-fought, with soldiers and armies returning to demilitarized zones to recoup and re-strategize. But, to win the war, one had to kill the king or capture the king. It didn't matter how many men had fallen in battle; if the king and a small contingent got away, they could regroup, re-direct their efforts, and hopefully come back stronger.

In chess, when the king is checkmated, the game is finished. Over. No more moves. For anyone. This is how important the king is.

Let's take a look at the rest our text in Exodus 1:17-20 (NLT)

But because the midwives feared God, they refused to obey the king's orders. They allowed the boys to live, too. So the king of Egypt called for the midwives. "Why have you done this?" he demanded. "Why have you allowed the boys to live?"

"The Hebrew women are not like the Egyptian women," the midwives replied. "They are more vigorous and have their babies so quickly that we cannot get there in time."

So God was good to the midwives, and the Israelites continued to multiply, growing more and more powerful. And because the midwives feared God, he gave them families of their own.

Taking it back a few notches, the beginning of the Book of Exodus gives us insight to where God's chosen people find themselves: in chaos, plunged into a world of darkness where they are enslaved, afflicted and oppressed. The Egyptians, who just a few chapters before, in the book of Genesis, had been saved from famine by Jewish Joseph, seemed to have conveniently forgotten all he had done for their nation, and now, under new rule, saw these Israelite descendants as a scourge to be exterminated. Everything that Joseph had established was overturned or eliminated, and as an undeserved reward, the Israelites now found themselves in their first exile. It is here that genocide became the order of the day.

One would think that, following Pharaoh's command, there would be a greater outcry, a rallying of fighting men, who would come together and form bands, or makeshift armies to fight this atrocity. But the Bible says nothing of this. It does not say anything of the fathers who were who were going to have their name and bloodline cut off; but it does mention a specific set of women. The midwives.

These are the invaluable women who for centuries have been intricately and intimately connected with childbirth. It is here, in this passage in Exodus, that we have our very first record of them and this vocation, in the form of Shifra and Puah. These two women would serve as two of the most powerful female leaders in Jewish history, setting an historical precedent for the midwife's inherent faith in God. They did not for one second entertain the idea of adhering to Pharaohs command, even though they knew that their defiance and disobedience would mean certain death. Despite the conditions of their captivity, it was more important to obey God, than to fear whatever Pharaoh could and would do to them

The Midrash, which is the classical collection of the Sages' homiletic teachings on the Torah, states that Shifra and Puah, in reward for their strength and obedience actually became partners with God in creation, granting life to the Jewish children. *God bestowed goodness upon the midwives, and the people multiplied and became very strong. It was because the midwives feared God that He made houses for them.* (Exodus 1:20-21) These *houses* were, in fact, dynasties born through them, which extended all the way to the King of Kings, Jesus Christ, by way of the royal bloodline of King David.

"Rabbi Shlomo Yitzchaki, a foremost commentator on the Torah and Talmud, and a leader of the Jewish community in Alsace-Lorraine discusses the word the Torah uses for 'midwife', stating that the word used is the 'intensive form' versus the passive. One form is used for a normal childbirth, while the other indicates a difficult birth requiring assistance from the midwife. So Shifrah and Puah did not simply assist in the birth of the redemption. Indeed, they hastened its coming."

"The redemption of the Jewish nation from the bondage of Egypt, and indeed the bondage of exile throughout time, is a direct result of the actions of the Jewish women of their time. According to the Talmud, it was in reward for the righteous women of that generation that Israel was redeemed from Egypt." (Both excerpts taken from: *The Untold Story of the Hebrew Midwives and the Exodus* Article by Nechama Rubinstein in TheJewishWoman.org)

Isn't this such a beautiful picture of the other facet of what it means to be a woman in the kingdom of God?

Now let's bring it home. In chess, as in the Word, the queen protects the king. Remember that translucent thread, I mentioned earlier? Well let's see where following it has taken us.

Protecting the king.

I think that you would agree with me when I say that we lack kings. We lack leaders. We lack warriors. We lack fighting men. This generation is directly affected by the generations that came before, and because the previous king has absconded, the kings-to-be are being silently killed.

175

At the time of writing this, our country is embroiled in a tumultuous outcry. Women and children are being violently killed and raped and trafficked, and there is no-one they can look to for help, because the protector has become the perpetrator. There is a combination of men who have willingly stepped away from what God has called them to be, and men who have been made to be redundant, inconsequential, unimportant, unwanted, and unneeded by a society of women who have replaced and displaced them. There are men who have been raised devoid of any idea that they are kings or kinsman redeemers. There are would-be kings who have been traded off to pharaohs, in exchange for improvised, crude, pseudo-marital partnerships, who in turn, become pharaohs themselves. There are men who lack back bone or conviction, who are being slapped around, babied, and coddled on one end, and made to bury their identity as they are robed in hashtags, for the sins of their gender, on the other end. Our kings have lost their identity. When the king does not know who he is, how can the kingdom prevail?

In this era rife with gender based violence, and all the hashtags that are shaping the narrative for the future of our sons, I for one, simply cannot do #menaretrash. I can do #thatmanistrash. That man who has raped a girl, or violated a woman, or harmed a child: THAT MAN IS TRASH. And even so, I need to believe that that man is redeemable against the backdrop of the shed blood of Jesus Christ.

I am raising a king. I cannot buy into the belief that all men are trash, and that all men need to rope themselves into that phrase. It does nothing for us as woman, or the victims and survivors, when the men who are not to blame take away all hope for better, by standing under that same umbrella. I'd sooner look for a man that says: "I am not trash. I am a king and I am a priest. I WILL stand for you and by you. I WILL protect you. You can count on the man God made me to be." Finding such a man will give my son someone good to be, someone worthy to emulate.

We have boys who have yet to become men, boys who are being raised by hurt, abandoned, broken, victimized women who need to know they are not the sum of a gender's atrocities. We cannot teach them that they are trash simply by way of being born male. We need to give them something greater to aspire to. We need to teach them to be the men society is lacking. We cannot punish our sons for the sins of the vile and wicked. We cannot punish good men for the acts of weak grotesque males who haven't a clue what a man is, who have never aspired to be men of courage and valour and, most importantly, men of God. I fear for my son and what he is to become if we rid society of the few good men by forcing them to label themselves as trash. Yes, evil does prevail when good men do nothing, but let's not chop the hands of the ones who are trying. I have known wretched detestable men who have caused great damage with unspeakable violation, but I have known good men too, and it's the good ones who have had longevity. The trashy ones came in, destroyed, violated, broke, stole, tried to kill and LEFT. Their piece in my life story was a one liner. I cannot give them my entire book, and I certainly won't give them my legacy in my son. One liner men. I say, just #cleanupthetrash. Our hashtags have ramifications far beyond trends on social media. Causes are worthwhile and necessary, but all these shape the future. Changing the future starts by changing this narrative.

This is where we find our translucent thread. While the body count of the women and children is very real, and nothing to be scoffed at, I believe that the real spiritual attack is not on us. The real attack is delivering the last few blows, demolishing the remaining men who could rise up as kings who might effect change. Satan's plan has always been a bee line for the throne and thus for anyone in line for it. Starting in Genesis.

Now the serpent was more subtle and crafty than any living creature of the field which the Lord God had made. And he [Satan] said to the woman, Can it really be that God has said, You shall not eat from every tree of the garden?

And the woman said to the serpent, We may eat the fruit from the trees of the garden, Except the fruit from the tree which is in the middle of the garden. God has said, You shall not eat of it, neither shall you touch it, lest you die.

But the serpent said to the woman, You shall not surely die, For God knows that in the day you eat of it your eyes will be opened, and you will be like God, knowing the difference between good and evil and blessing and calamity. (Genesis 3:1- 5 AMPC)

Eve had no desire to *be like God*; all she had was a curiosity, and a misunderstanding. There is no record of God speaking directly to her about not eating the fruit; that's why the serpent could subtly come in with *did God really say?* Being like God was *his* desire, it was *his* aim, and somehow he made it seem like something she should want.

How you are fallen from heaven, O Lucifer, son of the morning! How you are cut down to the ground, You who weakened the nations! For you have said in your heart: "I will ascend into heaven, I will exalt my throne above the stars of God; I will also sit on the mount of the congregation on the farthest sides of the north; I will ascend above the heights of the clouds, I will be like the Most High." (Isaiah 14:12-14 NKJV)

Satan knew from the beginning that Eve (woman) was the gateway to Adam(man), and that man(the second Adam) is the gateway to God (John 14:6). It was through woman that he orchestrated the fall of man, and man's separation from God. When he realized that God already had a plan of redemption in place to reconcile man to himself,

Satan then went to the next rung up the ladder to the throne – Jesus

Then Jesus was led (guided) by the [Holy] Spirit into the wilderness (desert) to be tempted (tested and tried) by the devil. And He went without food for forty days and forty nights, and later He was hungry. And the tempter came and said to Him, If You are God's Son, command these stones to be made [loaves of] bread. But He replied, It has been written, Man shall not live and be upheld and sustained by bread alone, but by every word that comes forth from the mouth of God.

Then the devil took Him into the holy city and placed Him on a turret (pinnacle, gable) of the temple sanctuary. And he said to Him, If You are the Son of God, throw Yourself down; for it is written, He will give His angels charge over you, and they will bear you up on their hands, lest you strike your foot against a stone.

Jesus said to him "On the other hand, it is written also, You shall not tempt, test thoroughly, or try exceedingly the Lord your God.

Again, the devil took Him up on a very high mountain and showed Him all the kingdoms of the world and the glory (the splendour, magnificence, pre-eminence, and excellence) of them. And he said to Him, These things, all taken together, I will give You, if You will prostrate Yourself before me and do homage and worship me.

Then Jesus said to him, Begone, Satan! For it has been written, You shall worship the Lord your God, and Him alone shall you serve.

Then the devil departed from Him, and behold, angels came and ministered to Him.

(Matthew 4:1-11 AMPC)

First, Satan came to Jesus as food, sustenance. It is not coincidental that he approached Eve with the same tactic. Appetite.

I believe this speaks to our appetites for our wants in Eve's case, and in our needs in Jesus' case. It's not for nothing that the world has coined the phrase, "The way to a man's heart is through his stomach." It's easy to deceive the heart of man when you have taken hold of his appetites.

Secondly Satan came to Eve in the form of an offer revealed in her new awakening. She would be like God. He approached Jesus in a different manner on the same matter, stating *"If you are the Son of God..."* This time he flips the coin and wants Jesus to reveal His Sovereignty at a time that was not appointed Him. If Jesus was indeed the 'Son of God'...

And thirdly he came to Eve as an enticement of power *"... knowing the difference between good and evil and blessing and calamity..."* Succumbing to this fruit, yielding to it, would endow her with knowledge she had not had before, empowering her. To Jesus he said, "Succumb to me, bow to me, and I will endow you with the power that comes from attainment of wealth and glory."

Every instance of these three presentations made to Eve and to Jesus, was made, and are being made to man. This exact argument that was sold to Eve, Eve sold to Adam. Adam knew that surely 'God did say', because God spoke directly to him, so he was enticed by the reasoning. The exchange.

I believe the three things that Satan presented to Jesus are the same things man is plagued with.

- Appetites (cravings, passions, inclinations, desires)

- Equality (being as God/being your own god). It is worthy to note that Jesus Himself, in his human form, did not think *this equality with God was a thing to be eagerly grasped or retained...* (Philippians 2:6)

- Power (by attainment of wealth and glory for self)

It is the poetry in God that is revealed as He bridges the gap that sin left open, and closes the circle again, excluding Satan, when Jesus says *"I am the way, the truth, and the life. No one comes to the Father except through Me."* (John 14:6) He brings direction back, He dispels the deception, and He resurrects, not with a wannabe resurrection, but the real deal.

Satan used Eve as the gateway to Adam, and God used the second Adam as a gateway to Himself.

I would like to put this to you: There is only one way to the Father, and that is through Jesus, but there are many ways to Jesus. One of those is woman.

I am calling on the midwife within you. Thank God for the midwives. The wives. The wives in the middle. The women. It is the wives in the middle who stand midway between the destroyer and the seed carrier, the women who won't go down without a fight. They do not take up arms, they take to their knees. They 'hold their position'.

If Pharaoh had known anything, he would have killed the midwives, because the queen protects the king. The midwife is the queen who stands between king and killer.

1 Samuel 19 tells the story of Michal, King David's wife and the daughter of ousted Saul. Many of us are only familiar with her as pertaining to her comment of the naked dancing David when he was already king, bringing back the ark of the covenant. I must say that I was among those who have written her off as a hindrance to the holy, but I have since recanted. Here we learn how Saul had planned to use this marriage as a means to kill David, but Saul had not factored in Michal's love for David, which is what made her a midwife, an intercessor, a gap stander.

Saul sent messengers that night to David's house to watch him, that he might kill him in the morning. But Michal, David's wife, told him, If you do not save your life tonight, tomorrow you will be killed.

So Michal let David down through the window, and he fled and escaped. And Michal took the teraph (household good luck image) and laid it in the bed, put a pillow of goats' hair at its head, and covered it with a bedspread.

And when Saul sent messengers to take David, she said, He is sick. (1 Samuel 19:11-14 AMPC)

Michal held her position as wife and took on the role of protector. She stood in harm's way and deceived the deceiver by lying about David's whereabouts. This picture is a reflection of the story of Rahab. Here Michal lets down the rope through the window, and sends her love, the rightful king, off to his safety in order to preserve his destiny.

Rewind to Joshua chapter 2, when a harlot named Rahab, lets down a scarlet rope, saving the lives of two spies and in so doing, preserves her destiny and secures her place in the lineage of the King of kings. But that's not all. Because Rahab stood midway between the king who needed to be dethroned and the new kingdom that needed to be established, she became the mother of the man all woman aspire to marry – Boaz.

I have not heard of any single Christian woman, who hasn't uttered the words that she is "waiting for her Boaz." Ruth didn't ever wait anywhere for anyone. She was spotted working in the field. She was blooming where she was planted.

Here's a clue ladies, your Kinsman Redeemer is a man of substance, looking for substance. You will only be noticed working in the field. If a Boaz is what you seek, then you won't find him looking cute 'up in da club', or on Tinder. You will find something, but not a Kinsman Redeemer. Ruth was working. You need to be working the field of where God has placed you.

Ruth was standing in the gap for her mother-in-law. She was holding back poverty and death from starvation with one hand, and working the field with the other. We see Ruth as an unlikely midwife, but here she is, coaxing Naomi to keep pushing, standing alongside her as though Naomi were travailing in childbirth in bitterness with a stillborn baby. Ruth stands midway between Naomi and hopelessness. The beauty of childbirth is the transition between labour and delivery those intense moments of pain and anguish, and work and sweat, and the joy and elation, release and relief of delivery.

Somewhere in this story, Ruth and Naomi swap roles and the midwife becomes the mother, and the mother, the midwife. As Ruth laboured in the sun, in the pain of the loss of her husband, and the sweat of her brow gathering left over grain, she transitioned into receiving a promise, in the form of a new husband, a special delivery from God – her Kinsman redeemer, Boaz. And in the progression of events, Naomi became the midwife guiding Ruth through the process and transition from grieving widow, to blushing bride. A beautiful portrait of gap-standing in the harem.

The story of Ruth and Boaz has many scholars arguing about whether or not Ruth was right in lying at Boaz's feet. Was it appropriate for her to 'woo him' as it were?

...the Lord has created a new thing in the land [of Israel]: a female shall compass (woo, win, and protect) a man (Jeremiah 31:22 AMPC).

Jeremiah 31 in its totality speaks of the glory of the new covenant that God makes with wayward returning Israel. As in the previous chapter the restoration of Judah is foretold, so in this is the restoration of Israel's ten tribes foretold. To read the chapter in its entirety is lengthy, yet meaty and satisfying with the revelation of prophecy for the children of God, and I believe it is a wonderful word for the women in these end times. I want to start with Verse 15, the same scripture we previously read in Matthew 2:16-18.

Thus says the LORD:

"A voice is heard in Ramah, lamentation and bitter weeping. Rachel is weeping for her children; she refuses to be comforted for her children, because they are no more."

Thus says the LORD:

"Keep your voice from weeping, and your eyes from tears, for there is a reward for your work, declares the LORD, and they shall come back from the land of the enemy. There is hope for your future, declares the LORD, and your children shall come back to their own country. Set up road markers for yourself; make yourself guideposts; consider well the highway, the road by which you went.

Return, O virgin Israel, return to these your cities. How long will you waver, O faithless daughter? For the LORD has created a new thing on the earth: a woman encircles a man. ... a female shall compass (woo, win, and protect) a man." (Jeremiah 31:15-22 ESV)

Chapter 12
CALL TO ARMS

*There's an echo in the emptiness, A Yearning in the stillness,
Hushed in silent expectation*

Awaiting in quiet times of revelation

*Predestined and set apart long before Prepared and trained
for this time of war*

Raised up only from the dust

No confidence in man, For in God we trust.

Destroyers of the stronghold Watch new warriors unfold

*Strong and steadfast, bold and unashamed Spirit of a
conqueror, No victory unattained. Clothed in purpose and guided
by grace*

Longing not for Gods hand, seeking only His face.

*A new generation, a whole new breed Passionate and Holy,
living by a different creed.*

*Pushing and pressing always onward Focused in Glory,
Leaning on God's Word.*

Armed for Action

Not caught in distraction Piercing eyes that see and know,

Deeper in knowledge, seeing more than what you show.

*Defined in each muscle, a soldiers form Strengthened in each
battle, though wounded and torn*

Fast and furious, Swift and steady

Not caught unaware, ever standing ready

*At the end of the isle, adorned in gold and in white The bride
kneels with tenderness, and arises with might*

*She takes up her sword, and with merging voices she sings,
The harem joins chorus as the battle cry begins*

Louder and louder they chant in the street

*No longer wailing their haunting melody of defeat They flutter
in formation, around the king and the son The lioness has
ascended, the fight has now begun!*

CALL TO ARMS

*Now gather yourself in troops, O daughter of troops; a state of
siege has been placed against us. They shall smite the ruler of Israel
with a rod (a scepter) on the cheek.* (Micah 5:1 Amplified Bible,
Classic Edition AMPC)

This Micah passage is a call to arms. It's a war cry to women. To daughters and to mothers and to wives to come to the aid of the king, of whom the enemy has made a mockery by slapping him in the face. Remember that woman is the gateway to man, so it stands to reason that she is his first line of defence. A siege has been placed against us.

We are surrounded and attacked from every side, and it seems in the natural that the fight is against us. But it's not. It never has been. The fight is for the seed carrier. The fight is for the male child. The fight is for the king.

The Message Bible says it like this:

But for now, prepare for the worst, victim daughter! The siege is set against us. They humiliate Israel's king, slapping him around like a rag doll.

For me, this Message version speaks more to where we are at now. This victim daughter – the ones being attacked, and the ones being raped, and killed and the ones being trafficked – these are the ones being commanded to attention. The victim is the daughter, but the target is the king.

Although this text is a prediction of the troubles and distresses of the Jewish nation and the promise of a Saviour, I want you to look at it as pertaining to what God is saying to us here and now. Let's imagine for a minute that Israel's king or the Ruler of Israel is a picture of man, of the male child, of the husband specifically.

When my mom and dad got married, my dad still wasn't saved. That didn't stop my mother from continuing to pray and believe for the man of promise she had asked God for. Every day she would continue to call him "pastor", much to his irritation. When he was laid up for hours reading his magazines she would say: "Thank You

Lord that my husband loves reading Your Word even more than he loves to read these magazines." When he would yell profanities at her, she would say "Thank You Lord, that my husband will speak Your Word to multitudes and that many will come to salvation." When they were in bed, she would reach over and anoint his head, pretending to stretch. She would call forth the man she knew he was. She wrote out scriptures and placed them under the inner soles of his shoes; she placed them in the pillowcase upon which he rested his head; she placed them under the bedsheet upon which they slept, and in the duvet cover that covered them. She was fighting for his soul like a spy in a foreign country. She did not hide her beliefs or her intentions. Her method was just incognito.

One day my mom got the news that her brother-in-law got saved and was baptized. She was livid! It's not that she wasn't happy for her sister or her brother-in-law's salvation, it was that she had been at the feet of the Lord too long for God not to have saved my dad's soul first. In her mind, this was unfair, and she was going to do something about it. When she heard, she called in to work as sick, took the day off and stayed home to go to war. That day she grabbed hold of Jesus, arresting Him for her situation.

She opened every window and every door and began sweeping, praying and crying as she swept. She swept out every desire in my dad that was in direct opposition to what she had asked God for. She swept out his magazines, and the cigarettes. She swept out the unproductive movie marathons he had on Friday nights. She swept out every inclination for a drop of alcohol. She swept and swept and prayed and cried.

When she was done, she invited the Holy Spirit to invade every corner and space in their home. She took out every single piece of clothing he owned, and laid it out, and anointed it with oil; she lay on them as she prayed and partnered with heaven for his soul. Then she left it with God.

Exactly three months later to the day, my dad had a sudden urge to get to the tent crusade hosted by Nicky Van Der Westhuizen Snr., and to give his life to the Lord. In a borrowed vehicle, in the dark of night, with two small children, he drove to the tent and made it just in time for the closing altar call. As my mom tells it, my dad parked the car haphazardly and ran down the dusty aisle and fell on his knees at the altar. That day my dad got saved. The very next day, he got rid of every ashtray in their home, and every bottle of alcohol, empty or not. My mom was shocked and a bit sceptical of what she was seeing, as though she had not urged God to intervene. She called my dad's smoking buddy at work and asked if he was smoking at work maybe, and his response pulled her into the reality of God. He said, "No. He has stopped smoking, broke almost every ashtray, and every morning we have to meet for morning devotion before we start work." This is God.

From then on, if you looked for my dad, his nose and entire being were caught up in reading the Bible, devouring its contents. And soon after he was preaching and leading many to salvation. Every opportunity he had, he spoke of salvation in Jesus Christ, and our weekends became occasions for outreach and open-air services. With a speaker, a microphone, and the Bible, he went about preaching the Word. All of this happened because my mom waged a war on her knees.

This is our battle. This is our mandate.

We need to affect change on a global scale, and that is not going to happen while we fight for the right to be equal to men. We were never called to be equal to men. We were called to be a helpmeet to them. A synonym for equal is identical. If there are two of the same, one is not needed. We don't need women who will fight as men do, we need women who will rise and awaken demoralized armies, women who fight differently.

I am reminded of Joan of Arc.

"Before the appearance of Joan of Arc... the French army had not achieved any major victories for a generation..." (Wikipedia)

France was divided into two factions, between the king's brother and the king's cousin. The king himself, Charles VI, was indisposed, as he suffered with bouts of insanity which often rendered him unable to rule.

"For generations, there had been prophecies in France which promised the nation would be saved by a virgin from the "borders of Lorraine" "who would work miracles" and "that France will be lost by a woman and shall thereafter be restored by a virgin." (Wikipedia Citation. Fraioli, Deborah. *Joan of Arc and the Hundred Years' War*, Westport: Greenwood Press, 2005. p.59)

This correlates directly with a quote by Saint Augustine: "By the fall a poison was handed to mankind through a woman [Eve], by the Redemption man was given salvation also through a woman [Mary]"

This strand of woman as key in redemption is intertwined with the translucent thread that led us to the killing of the king. Revelation 12 speaks of it as well, in a time that is yet to come, and a prophecy that is yet to unfold.

And a great sign (wonder)—[warning of future events of ominous significance] appeared in heaven: a woman clothed with the sun, with the moon under her feet, and with a crownlike garland (tiara) of twelve stars on her head. She was pregnant and she cried out in her birth pangs, in the anguish of her delivery.

Then another ominous sign (wonder) was seen in heaven: Behold, a huge, fiery-red dragon, with seven heads and ten horns, and seven kingly crowns (diadems) upon his heads. His tail swept [across the sky] and dragged down a third of the stars and flung them to the earth. And the dragon stationed himself in front of the woman who was about to be delivered, so that he might devour her child as soon as she brought it forth.

And she brought forth a male Child, One Who is destined to shepherd (rule) all the nations with an iron staff (scepter), and her Child was caught up to God and to His throne.

And the woman [herself] fled into the desert (wilderness), where she has a retreat prepared [for her] by God, in which she is to be fed and kept safe for 1,260 days (42 months; three and one-half years).

Then war broke out in heaven; Michael and his angels went forth to battle with the dragon, and the dragon and his angels fought. But they were defeated, and there was no room found for them in heaven any longer. And the huge dragon was cast down and out— that age-old serpent, who is called the Devil and Satan, he who is the seducer (deceiver) of all humanity the world over; he was forced out and down to the earth, and his angels were flung out along with him.

Then I heard a strong (loud) voice in heaven, saying, Now it has come—the salvation and the power and the kingdom (the dominion, the reign) of our God, and the power (the sovereignty, the authority) of His Christ (the Messiah); for the accuser of our brethren, he who keeps bringing before our God charges against them day and night, has been cast out! And they have overcome (conquered) him by means of the blood of the Lamb and by the utterance of their testimony, for they did not love and cling to life even when faced with death [holding their lives cheap till they had to die for their witnessing]. Therefore be glad (exult), O heavens and you that dwell in them! But woe to you, O earth and sea, for the devil has come down to you in fierce anger (fury), because he knows that he has [only] a short time [left]!

And when the dragon saw that he was cast down to the earth, he went in pursuit of the woman who had given birth to the male Child. But the woman was supplied with the two wings of a giant eagle, so that she might fly from the presence of the serpent into the desert (wilderness), to the retreat where she is to be kept safe and fed for a time, and times, and half a time (three and one-half years, or 1,260 days).

Then out of his mouth the serpent spouted forth water like a flood after the woman, that she might be carried off with the torrent. But the earth came to the rescue of the woman, and the ground opened its mouth and swallowed up the stream of water which the dragon had spouted from his mouth. So then the dragon was furious (enraged) at the woman, and he went away to wage war on the remainder of her descendants—[on those] who obey God's commandments and who have the testimony of Jesus Christ [and adhere to it and bear witness to Him]. (Revelation 12:1-17 Amplified Bible, Classic Edition AMPC)

This seems to be a recurring theme. Verses 4, 5, 13 and v.17

...And the dragon stationed himself in front of the woman who was about to be delivered, so that he might devour her child as soon as she brought it forth.

And she brought forth a male Child, One Who is destined to shepherd (rule) all the nations with an iron staff (scepter)...

And when the dragon saw that he was cast down to the earth, he went in pursuit of the woman who had given birth to the male Child.

So then the dragon was furious (enraged) at the woman and went away to wage war on the remainder of the descendants...

The devil is after the Son that is born, and when he can't lay hold of him, he goes in pursuit of the woman. The devil was after Adam, so he went in pursuit of Eve. He was after Moses so he went in pursuit of the midwives, trying to get them to do his bidding.

Let's go back to our foundation scripture for this section (Jeremiah 31:15 ESV): *Thus says the LORD: A voice is heard in Ramah, lamentation and bitter weeping. Rachel is weeping for her children; she refuses to be comforted for her children, because they are no more.*

This was the scripture foretelling the killing of the male child at Jesus' birth, and what would happen subsequent to that, yet it is also a prophecy for today. But to understand it in its entirety we need to ask certain questions, like: who is Rachel? And why is she mentioned in this New Testament passage?

The Rachel spoken of here, is the same Rachel found in Genesis, married to Jacob. What we know of Rachel is that she so desired to have children that she considered herself dead without them. (Genesis 30:1) Many commentaries on the above scripture believe that Jeremiah was speaking figuratively, as Rachel is represented as crying from her grave.

The key words that tie the prophecy of old with the generation we are in, come from verses Jeremiah 31:16 – 17, 21b and 22.

Thus says the LORD:

"Keep your voice from weeping, and your eyes from tears, for there is a reward for your work, {your endurance will be rewarded-Common English Bible} declares the LORD, and they shall come back from the land of the enemy."

But the Lord says: "Don't cry any longer for I have heard your prayers, and you will see them again; they will come back to you from the distant land of the enemy. There is hope for your future, declares the LORD, and your children shall come back to their own country.

"Set up road markers for yourself; make yourself guideposts; consider well the highway, the road by which you went. Return, O virgin Israel, return to these your cities.

How long will you waver, O faithless daughter? For the LORD has created a new thing on the earth: a woman encircles a man. /...a female shall compass (woo, win, and protect) a man." (Jeremiah 31:16, 17, 21b, 22 TLB)

My own personal commentary on this passage reads as follows:

There is an instruction to the women to stop wailing for the lost men, to stop sitting hopeless as though they were irredeemable, to dry their tears and prepare for the return of the male child, who will return from the land in which he is exiled. Jehovah gives assurance that the children, the sons, will return.

But what ensures their return is the prayers prayed by the woman, the wives, the daughters, the midwives, for God has heard their prayers. Their act of intercession, as standing midway between hopelessness and the end of posterity, has caught the attention of God, who has now promised a reward for their endurance, and faithfulness. The passage goes on to pledge that not only will this generation be saved, but so will the lineage coming from them. Their future is secure.

God then calls on a new wave of woman, whom he rebukingly calls virgin, denoting that she must once again make herself pure and Holy before God. This is the second chance brigade. The ones whom God is giving the opportunity to come alongside those who have already been praying. Consecrate yourself! Return to God and be faithful to His Word and His Kingdom, you young daughter who has compromised in the modern age. For the Lord needs you now to protect the man. Encompass him. Woo him back to his rightful place. It's time to gear up for battle.

Now gather yourself in troops, O daughter of troops... (Micah 5:1)

This war – to take back the kingdom, and to restore the king to his rightful place – has now fallen on the daughters of the kingdom. The 'daughters' speaks of a new generation. This is not a one-woman task. It's about gathering in troops.

The Cambridge English Dictionary defines troop as '...soldiers on duty in a large group.'

There was a time when a single woman arose in courage, and saved a nation, such as in the case of Esther and Joan of Arc, but now we need a contingent of women who will rise up together, stand as a troop, and fight as soldiers on their knees. We are now on duty. We are the new breed of army. Who is this army? What does she look like?

God imprinted in my spirit to look up what a 'samurai' is. According to Wikipedia, the Samurai were the military nobility

.... of medieval and early modern Japan. In Japanese they are referred to as bushi meaning 'warrior' or buke. According to translator William Scott Wilson: "In Chinese the character was originally a verb meaning 'to wait upon', 'accompany persons' in the upper ranks of society and this is also true of the original term in Japanese, saburau. In both countries the terms were nominalized to mean 'those who serve in close attendance to the nobility'..."

"...The samurai were usually associated with a clan, and their lord, and were trained as officers in military tactics and grand strategy."

– Wikipedia.org (Samurai)

"Originally, samurai were expected to be proficient in many weapons, as well as unarmed combat, and attain the highest possible mastery of combat skills. Ordinarily, the development of combative techniques is intertwined with the tools used to execute those techniques. In a rapidly changing world, those tools are constantly changing, requiring that the techniques to use them be continuously reinvented." – Wikipedia.org (Martial Arts)

"Maintaining the household was the main duty of women of the samurai class. This was especially crucial during early feudal Japan, when warrior husbands were often traveling abroad or engaged in clan battles. The wife, or okugatasama (meaning: one who remains in the home), was left to manage all household affairs, care for the children, and perhaps even defend the home forcibly. For this reason, many women of the samurai class were trained in wielding a polearm called a naginata or a special knife called the kaiken in an art called tantojutsu (lit. the skill of the knife), which they could use to protect their household, family, and honour if the need arose. There were women who actively engaged in battles alongside male samurai in Japan, although most of these female warriors (Onna-bugeisha) were not formal samurai.

Traits valued in women of the samurai class were humility, obedience, self-control, strength, and loyalty. Ideally, a samurai wife would be skilled at managing property, keeping records, dealing with financial matters, educating the children (and perhaps servants as well), and caring for elderly parents or in-laws that may be living under her roof. Confucian law, which helped define personal relationships and the code of ethics of the warrior class required that a woman show subservience to her husband, filial piety to her parents, and care to the children." – Wikipedia.org (Onna-bugeisha)

My research, while limited to Wikipedia, told me everything I needed to know pertaining to how this new generation of combatant brides is to wage the war.

Firstly, we need to understand and acknowledge that we serve in close attendance to the nobility. This means that the man lying on the couch watching his soccer or rugby may not look like much to you, but he is the nobility you are called to serve in close attendance to. For the unmarried, it's seeing the opposite sex, not as the prized husband to be obtained to escape singleness, but as the king that God sees, understanding that your role is one of service. Not servitude, but service.

Secondly, you need to be trained. You're not going into this war with a long-range missile or snipers' gun. It's going to cost proximity in the fight. You are going to have to become proficient in military tactics, and that means knowing your enemy, pre-empting the attack, and by precision prayer, warding off the unseen strike. You need to have a strategy going in, and that means knowing the weapons needed in every scale of attack.

For the weapons of our warfare are not carnal but mighty in God for pulling down strongholds... (2 Corinthians 10:5 (NKJV).

That's the first line of offense. Getting the stronghold. We no longer fight from a position of defence, but of offense, knowing which weapon to use going in, and how to tap into and implore for the help you need. You cannot be calling on Jehovah Jireh, God our Provider, when the enemy comes in like a flood. You need to know that, at that point, you enlist the Sovereignty of Jehovah Sabaoth or Tzva'ot – the God of Armies or the Lord of Hosts of armies. You need to know your God. You need to have a working knowledge of the written Word of God, and the experience of the manifested Word made alive in your life – your testimony.

...casting down argument and every high thing that exalts itself against the knowledge of God, bringing every thought into captivity to the obedience of Christ, and being ready to punish all disobedience when your obedience is fulfilled. (2 Corinthians 10:5b-6 NKJV)

You need to be disciplined in strategy, and patient in surveillance. You need to have endurance to keep on the directed course of action, even when you don't understand the command, or see the results in the natural. You obey because your Commander in Chief, your Captain of the Hosts, Jesus, wills it so. You need to be able to break the fights within the factions, and to rebuke the rebellion of your own thoughts. You need to strive for your obedience in all aspects, removing the log from your own eye, before attempting the speck in your partner's. That is introspection and continual dying to self and continual repentance, giving no room for the enemy to grab a foothold.

You need to be trained in all manner of combat, and understand the signs of the times, so that you can apply the tools to the period, reinventing the technique. Changing the method but not the message.

Thirdly, there is nothing obvious and exposed about the Samurai. No tell-tale signs that they are indeed built for the fight, or that they are currently at war. Despite what we came to see on television, the Samurai did not walk around marked as 'secret elite'; that would have defeated their purpose entirely.

It's like this: You don't see Samurais walking around daily, just randomly handing out karate chops and flying kicks, and waving their mighty swords atop their heads. No. But they are still Samurai and they are still out there. You don't see these flexible, agile beings jumping from rooftops and scaling trees, as they try to make their way down the street. No, they are incognito, inconspicuous but still deadly, highly trained, focused masters of their art. They bear the seal of their clan or their lord.

"They are not of the world, even as I am not of the world. Sanctify them in the truth; Your word is truth. As You sent Me into the world, I also have sent them into the world. For their sakes I sanctify Myself, that they themselves also may be sanctified in truth. I do not

ask on behalf of these alone, but for those also who believe in Me through their word; that they may all be one; even as You, Father, are in Me and I in You, that they also may be in Us, so that the world may believe that You sent Me." (John 17:16-21 NASB)

That's who you should be. In union and in unity with your Commander in Chief, and in unity with the contingent of soldiers alongside whom you stand, fight and serve, bearing the seal of your clan, projecting the image of your Lord. No attention, glory or fame is focused on self. It's about the greater mandate and executing your orders, understanding that you do not fight as the world fights, but as highly trained demon assassins. *For though we walk in the flesh, we do not war according to the flesh* (2 Corinthians 10:3 NKJV).

The Samurai women are awfully close to the Proverbs 31 wife in description. She does not neglect her other duties, but she has also been skilled in the art of war and can fight alongside her husband in partnership, as one. The Samurai woman can hold the fort, and give her man some recovery time, but she can also take a page from David's book and encourage her own self, should the need arise. She is not nipping at his heels, causing division within. "It's one thing if the devil is an outsider, but an entirely different prayer game if the devil is one, or a group in your life." This is a quote and piece of advice from my dear friend's mother. It is so apt and applies as much within the marital union as it does to those surrounding the marital union.

Since we are speaking of a troop, this assignment is not a lone mission. It requires arming the women of the harem. It requires the unity of an armed force, with one common goal – the reinstating of the King. It's not about female empowerment. It's about all those things that mothers are. Your mother will root for you, and fight for you, and stand by you, and at no point, is she trying to be what you are called to be. She'll push you into that thing and believe against all odds for you, but never steal your crown. That's the selfless beauty of the maternal. Being a trooper in this battle means we harness everything that makes us feminine, and makes us women, and use those things as tools in our arsenal to wage a war to which we have been called as covert officers.

We band together, in unity, as individuals who stand in the gaps in our homes, with the full force of the harem as our spiritual backing.

The dichotomy of this army, is the contrast between warrior and Bride, and between the existing unity of the whole, and the stand of the individual in her home. This woman is not alone. She stands as part of a Holy Harem, and she understands that in her individuated capacity she stands taller on her knees. I call this woman, not just a warrior, but a bride in the detail. Not just a bride, but a Samurai in the fight. She is not a bride for a Samurai. She is a Samurai. She is a bride. Fully warrior/ soldier/ trooper. Fully unblemished, prepared, ready bride. Samurai Bride!

www.ingramcontent.com/pod-product-compliance
Lightning Source LLC
Chambersburg PA
CBHW032225080426
42735CB00008B/721